Jacqueline,

Dr. Ruth

Women Create!

Women Create!

A seriously whimsical celebration
of the creative feminine

Hilda Ruch

BROWN BOOKS
PUBLISHING GROUP

Women Create!

A Seriously Whimsical Celebration of the Creative Feminine

Manufactured in the United States of America

For information, please contact:
Brown Books Publishing Group
16200 North Dallas Parkway, Suite 170
Dallas, Texas 75248
www.brownbooks.com
972-381-0009
A New Era in Publishing™

ISBN-13: 978-1-934812-15-0
ISBN-10: 1-934812-15-3
LCCN: 2008926922
1 2 3 4 5 6 7 8 9 10

Dedication

*To all of the women I know and love
and to those I have yet to meet.*

Table of Contents

Acknowledgments

Through several years *Women Create!* nourished my creativity, stirred my sense of wonder, and provided countless opportunities to learn. Thanks a million to all who joined me in my happy writing project. So many wonderful cohorts were always helpful and inspiring, providing aid, comfort, and encouragement. Thanks to each of you, you know who you are. You listened to me yak about creativity, women, and all I had to discover about getting a book published. You helped shape and hone a cluster of ideas and assumptions into *Women Create*!

A big happy thank you goes to Brown Books Publishing Group. With quintessential wild women creativity, Milli Brown lights up the publishing world. Milli, I thank you so much for caring about this book. Kathryn Grant and Janet Harris skillfully organized and guided the book through the publication process and gave beautiful form to my manuscript. Ted Ruybal knows his way around a dust jacket and book design. "Pow, off the shelves!" Cindy Birne and Cathy Williams read you like a book. Their enthusiastic approach to public relation and marketing is flawlessly personalized. BBPG rocks. Your attention, passion, and precision were unstinting. Thank you!

To Gina Mazza Hillier, my perfect editor, thank you for your thoughtful, tender, and timely commentary. You encouraged me to make my book better and tried to tame my wild enthusiasm for quotes.

I am forever indebted to the bounteous wisdom and quick-witted eloquence of women. I thought a few pointed quotes appropriately scattered throughout the book might be a good idea. But as I searched written materials and Web sites, I discovered more and more spirited, poignant, elegant, and funny quotable notable women. The muse of creative whimsy took over and hundreds of quotes found a home in *Women Create!*

The notable quotable quotations were a hoot to research, choose, and place. They underpin the text with women's unique attitudes, styles, and insights. Support for ideas, surprising combinations, emotional depth, and beautiful words were some of the selection criteria. I endeavored to use small, but powerful excerpts in a transformative way to provide social commentary on women's creative spirit.

Acknowledgments

I've tried to find the most authentic version of the hundreds of quotations that so felicitously support my thoughts about women and creativity. It is possible that some mistakes, inaccuracies, or incorrect attributions have occurred. I've provided brief descriptions of the source for each example of feminine common sense, intelligence, and brilliance.

Thank you to Sharon Bailey, Molly Bogen, Regen Fearon, Susybelle Gosslee, Hedy Helsell, Judy Keith, Jean Keller, Pat Mattingly, Jennifer Nagorka, Nancy Solana, Susan Stahl, and Connie Wilson. This fabulous group read and critiqued the wild women interview protocol. They invested time in reading the questionnaire and giving me suggestions for making it a better process. Each of these catalysts shared something from her understanding and beliefs, enriching mine twelve-fold. Their bounteous spirits of giving were angel dusted with humor, candor, courage, and connection.

Here is to Cherette, Cindy, Cynthia, Diane, Elba, Elizabeth, Harriet, Jane, Jennifer, Mary, Pam, Pat, Peggy, Penny, Regina, Rena, and Terri, the colorful, talented, and best ever wild women. Thank you for your compelling stories. Your insights and experiences underscore the powerful diversity that ranges through creative thought and expression. Each story is meant to highlight the steeliness, courage, humor, talents, and gifts that you shared with me. Within the limitations of the artfulness of my writing, I hope only to give strength to my connections with you generous and wise women and to share your creativity with all who read this book. Y'all were eloquent.

With love and a million thanks to Mom, Dad, and Senior, they nurtured and supported my creative whimsy. Together they created a family where I never learned I couldn't be creative!

I saved the last and most heartfelt thank you for the best. That would be Kent Skipper, great husband, terrific colleague, and totally cool friend. He ever-lovingly and thoughtfully spent time discussing my wild conjurings, concerns, and challenges. He endlessly reviewed drafts and was always ready to listen to my exuberant and often carried-away intensity for everything female and creative. At all times, he kept me going with his interest and understanding. Forever encouraging, his support buoyed and nurtured me and *Women Create*! He loved the quotes and encouraged me to squeeze in some more. One bodacious and undaunted guy!

Foreword

After a successful career as an educational leader and family therapist, Dr. Hilda Ruch embarked on a new path to be a writer and voice for the creativity she has observed in women. Throughout this entertaining and original work, she encourages readers to explore and affirm their creativity. The spontaneity, humor, and profound understanding in these pages reflect the author herself.

I had the honor of being introduced to Hilda through a mutual friend who thought since we were both writing a book we should get together. The first time I met her, I was left with no doubt she had a passion for and great depth of knowledge about women and creativity. I can hear her energetic voice and feel her vibrant enthusiasm as I write about *Women Create! A Seriously Whimsical Celebration of the Creative Feminine.*

My pleasure in inviting you to read this book comes from knowing the author. Her unstoppable enthusiasm evokes new appreciation for creativity and the ways it enhances life. Hilda's quick flow of ideas and images are enlivened by her engaging style. With unique ingenuity she integrates her rich career experiences of thirty years with the brilliance and gumption of hundreds of women . . . famous, infamous, past, present, fictional, and the totally real thing.

With resilient nature and embracing nurture, women shape culture and history and enrich the world. Read and be a part of an intimate, engaging, humorous, inspiring, and downright friendly book. Discover that being creative is a part of being human. See how creativity impacts our lives and the way we live. Connecting, learning, achieving, and leading are explored as basic arenas for using, strengthening, and embellishing creativity. Hilda inspires us to recognize and use our creativity to jazz up our unique strength, humor, and resilience. She paints a dynamic vision of human creativity and makes it accessible.

Each reader will recognize something different and create her own insights. Appreciate and celebrate your personal creative feminine and recognize her in other women. Perhaps understand why we use it in one area of life more than another or spot aspects of creativity that we would like to nurture. While you're reading *Women Create!*, you will catch glimpses of your own creativity, whimsy, and wisdom. Proclaim your fascinating creativity; transform possibility into exhilarating reality.

Women Create! weaves interviews, quotes, historical vignettes, personal stories, and fictional icons to create a kaleidoscopic picture of women's creative enterprises. No instructions, to do lists or tests ... imagination and creativity are free to mix, match, pick, and choose. Each reader will find new paths to confirm, encourage, and embolden creativity. Be warned—this is not a "how to" book. Rather, it's a "why not" book! Be prepared to soar as you get in touch with your own unique and ever-present creative feminine.

Nancy Barry

Motivational speaker

Author of *When Reality Hits: What Employers Want Recent College Graduates to Know*

Chapter One

Creativity

I am not an eccentric. It's just that I am more alive than most people.
I am an unpopular electric eel in a pond of goldfish.

—Dame Edith Sitwell, English poet, critic, biographer

In order to be irreplaceable, one must always be different.

—Coco Chanel, French fashion icon

*L*ights, camera, action! Cinema legend Mary Pickford embodies the notions of celebrity and superstar. America's Sweetheart invented the image of the spunky girl next door and perfected the portrayal of everyman's first love. She got her start on Broadway, but found her true passion in Hollywood.

Mary Pickford's life story is a glorious tale of soaring creativity. As an actor, director, executive producer, and studio owner, she mastered the many facets of success in the newfound empire of Hollywood in the 1900s. With take-charge vitality, Pickford presided over all aspects of making, producing, and distributing her films. She hired talent and crew. She influenced scripting, editing, release, and promotion. Pickford defined film acting and set the standard for filmmaking. Her films are among the best to come out of Tinseltown.

Pickford's philosophy in a nutshell: "It is not my prerogative as an actress to teach the public anything. They will teach me . . . I am a servant of the public. I have never forgotten that." Pickford acted in more than 200 films in thirty-six years, had creative control over every facet of her career, and was the first female actor to earn more than a million dollars per year. She was the premiere actor to leave her handprints and footprints at Grauman's Chinese Theater. What's more, Pickford was one of the three co-founders of

United Artists and one of the thirty-six founders of the Academy of Motion Picture Arts and Sciences. Her philosophy worked.

Wow! Pickford knew how to put her creative feminine to work. As a beacon for all women, her life is a celebration of creative spirit. Like Pickford, creativity is a white-hot star glowing in the heaven of human potential. Creativity illuminates the complexity of the human psyche and shimmers with the aura of unique self-expression.

What is this thing called creativity? It is a universal aspect of human nature, a part of being alive, and the ultimate expression of being human. The notion that creative ability is a rare commodity among just a few great artists is a myth. Everyone has creative potential, and I have come to believe that it is basic to our nature and essential to our identity. The creative feminine, in particular, lives in our capacity to imagine and leap to insight. She pulses through our physical, cognitive, cultural, and spiritual being, stimulating excitement and the urge to fulfill our dreams. Creativity is a complex marvel, difficult to describe. Creativity begins its life as a synaptic flash in the brain. Chemical and electrical signals emit sensations that conjure ideas and spur activities. Sometimes when my creative feminine is on a tear, I can actually feel the zing of wild, unleashed ideas generating inside my head.

Life provides opportunities to adapt, innovate, and stir up a bit of razzmatazz. Our days are chock-full of opportunities for creative expression. French author, Sidonie Gabrielle Claudine Colette, put it this way: "You will do foolish things, but do them with enthusiasm." My own creative feminine loves the siren call of a new challenge. In my wild woman moments, I can sense the arrival of the madcap energy of psyched up creativity. My creative feminine and I are going to raise a rumpus!

When the creative feminine comes to call, it is good to have a space of your own to receive her. The following three stories relate a woman's need for a room of her own. Former First Lady Pat Nixon said, "I'll have to have a room of my own. Nobody could sleep with Dick. He wakes up during the night, switches on the lights, and speaks into his tape recorder." Feminist icon, Virginia Stephen Woolf, voiced the idea perfectly: "A woman must have money and a room of her own if she is to write fiction." The third example is my own. While writing this book, I decided that what had been a TV room and office needed to become a woman-at-work place. About two years ago, I had ripped out a magazine page that was saturated with a most magnificently vibrant shade of red. From time to time, I would think that it would be a spectacular room color. In a flash of "What took you so long?" the color became mine. Velvety, vivid paint, a removed wall, and French doors transformed the room. Now, happily at work, I bask in my light-infused red room. Thank you, Pat and Virginia.

I have always loved Holly Golightly and her carefree, yet sensitive, style. Her story speaks to the notion that we all have the creative muscle to shape our lives. You can sense the creative feminine moxie at work when Holly says, "Let me tell you something, mister. If I had her money, I'd be richer than she is."

✑ Holly Golightly ✑

Never born, she will always live.

Window shopping at Tiffany's early in the morning, getting $50 for the powder room, or innocently delivering messages between an imprisoned mobster and his lawyer, Holly Golightly makes her own way with sophisticated naiveté. She thrives on doing things she has never done before. Not knowing does not scare her, it invites her to explore and expand her horizons.

Holly can get dressed in an elegant flash and hail a New York taxi even quicker. A whimsically pragmatic nonesuch, she magically defines and redefines her image. Behind the quirky façade is a seriously independent woman. The world belongs to Holly.

—From *Breakfast at Tiffany's*, the 1961 movie based on Truman Capote's 1958 novella of the same name

Like Holly, we display our creativity to suit our distinctive needs. Creative potential increases with attention. Every day shines with opportunities to benefit from this boundless asset. Cooking, for instance, is ripe with daily occasions for creative responses. For me, a day spent writing can mean *What in the world will I make for dinner?* Reservations are not always the best answer. Creativity comes to the rescue. Eggs, cream, and frozen spinach lurk in the refrigerator. Good. Chicken stock and saffron beckon from the pantry. Excellent. The meal unfolds as a simple omelet and cream of spinach soup with a saffron swirl. Deliciously redeemed, I can make reservations tomorrow.

The creative feminine shapes perspective and supports endeavors. We often create options and responses to life as we live it. Life throws curves. Michele, in *Romy and Michele's High School Reunion*, spins the curve right back when she says to Romy, her best friend, "You know, even though I had to wear that stupid back brace and you were kind of fat, we were still totally cutting edge." Throw a fastball at Pat Schroeder, former member of U.S. Congress, and she will knock it out of the ballpark. Here is one of her home runs: "When people ask me why I am running as a woman, I always answer, 'What choice do I have?'"

Emphasizing the personal twists inherent in creative expression, Pulitzer Prize-winning journalist Ellen Goodman told this story about Golda Meir. During a wave of crimes against women in Israel, a council of men asked Meir to put a nighttime curfew on females. Her response was a direct "No way." Her creative feminine inspired reasoning: If men were the problem, let the council enforce a curfew against *them*.

Creativity does not exist in universally generic templates but in the singular capacity of humans to imagine, intuit, adapt, innovate, risk, and persevere. The whorls and ridges of creative expression are imbedded in individual fingerprints of idiosyncrasy, ability, and talent. Creativity refuses to be contained in a single definition or measured in standardized assessments. Each person has an idea about what creativity is, how it is engaged, and the way it is expressed. Illustrator Mary Ellen Kelly captured the personal perspective of creativity: "Natives who beat drums to drive off evil spirits are objects of scorn to smart Americans who blow horns to break up traffic jams."

Creativity is a fabulously generous resource that replenishes itself and is enhanced through awareness and use. It annexes original ideas, numerous viewpoints, and uncommon combinations and animates ideas with humor, intuition, and imagination. Creativity is an everyday process and an acquired art that moves audaciously beyond certainties, vacating comfortable ruts and sure things.

Through many years of researching, playing with, and being fascinated by creativity, I have uncovered a really cool and deeply guarded secret: Creativity makes stuff up! Good old creativity knows that questions have scads of answers, problems have oodles of solutions, and quests have oceans of destinations. Creative instinct ignores formulas by recognizing infinite options. Innovation and pragmatism reside compatibly; paradoxical solutions coexist. Journalist Shana Alexander put it this way: "The paradox of reality is that no image is as compelling as the one which exists only in the mind." Creative process set aflame by freedom is not extinguished by constraint. Fostered by play, it is not stifled by rules. Untamed by accomplishment, creativity seeks new challenges.

Louise Nevelson made stuff up. As a pioneer of environmental sculpture, Nevelson was an independent artist who thrived on new ideas, disdained restrictions, and ignored confinement. Her materials included architectural debris, odd pieces of wood, cast metal, found objects, and everyday discards. Nevelson constructed wood boxes and assemblages; she stacked complex, rhythmic shapes into enormous interlocking masses and towering freestanding walls. She said, "When you put things together that other people have thrown out, you're really bringing them to life—a spiritual life that surpasses the life for which they were originally created."

Nevelson was a larger-than-life sculptor who created larger-than-life sculptures. Tall, thin, flamboyantly dressed and fluttering dazzlingly long, false eyelashes, she personified her creations. Her surreal whimsy and evocative ingenuity remain alive in her works. She made the creative process sound easy: "You must say to yourself, 'I feel like doing so and so.' I think it's that simple."

Clearly, Nevelson was one of a kind, and her work brilliantly represents her uniqueness. Same for each of us? Absolutely! Creative expression is personal and takes on original forms. Each spring I watch my university students work on their semester-long project, creating a biography. My syllabus outlines criteria for content and a few essential components, but subject, length, and manner of presentation are determined by each student's creative muse. Initially, students will ask what I want, but as the semester unfolds and they tap into their biography subject, creative juju flows. All manner of individual format, details, and adjunct materials begin to appear. The creative process fills my classroom.

The unruly process of creating defies simple models and descriptions. Like an armful of Slinkies, creativity has little regard for ordered steps. Creativity is a whirl of phases and sequences. We are in many loops of the process concurrently.

Brainstorming with others primes the creative pump. Notions and ideas trickle, spatter, and gush. Speculation, unhampered by evaluation and convention, can rush like an untamed river. Spontaneous conversation enriches the flood of possibilities. Free-flow ponderings produce varied and novel approaches. As we blend our ideas with others', creativity floats into an increasingly greater ocean of ideas.

At some point we want quality control. We need to identify the best ideas from our divergent, bubbled-up schemes and notions. In this phase of the creative process, we appraise the outflow of divergent thinking and unite the best-of-the-best into a common focus. The practical side of creativity—yes, it has a practical side—channels the flow.

In moving closer to our vision, new combinations of notions and speculations must be coaxed into harmony. Creativity unifies, integrates, and consolidates. Its flexibility reconfigures, realigns, and synthesizes diverse concepts. Author Denise Shekerjian touches on the mix-mingle-and-merge characteristics of creativity. "The person who can combine frames of reference and draw conclusions between ostensibly unrelated points of view is likely to be the one who makes the creative breakthrough." As an amalgam of knowledge, experience, and trial and error, creativity engages the imagination and stimulates improvisation.

Once the product of our efforts is at hand, creativity checks for feasibility and accommodates feedback before implementation. Pragmatic creativity survives second and third looks. Resilient creativity fine-tunes, amends, and surveys. Canny, sharp-eyed appraisal provides opportunities to adjust, touch-up, and edit. Enlightened editing brings elegance and practicality to creative works. Feminist writer Dorothy Bryant pinpointed the pot-of-gold reward that comes with the completion of creative endeavors when she wrote, "Like an old gold-panning prospector, you must resign yourself to digging up a lot of sand from which you will later patiently wash out a few minute particles of gold ore."

INSPIRED

All my concerts had no sounds in them; they were completely silent. People had to make up their own music in their minds.
—Yoko Ono, artist, entrepreneur

To seize the flying thought before it escapes us is our only touch with reality.
—Ellen Glasgow, American novelist

Creativity shines throughout life with energy and purpose. Like the moon, it holds sway over whimsy, conjecture, and analysis. The muse of inspiration sustains creative hoopla by infusing our efforts and aspirations with energy.

Molly Ivins, Texas high priestess of shoot-from-the hip journalism, was enlivened by what knocked others off their feet. Ivins worked as a columnist, commentator, raconteur, and author. Her motto? "Raise more hell." This feisty Texan loved words. She had a colorful, irreverent, and inventive way with the English language. Molly knew how to impale arrogance and pretension with hilarious, insightful wordplay. "I believe that ignorance is the root of all evil. And that no one knows the truth." When it came to political folly, she went for the jugular. "Next time I tell you someone from Texas should not be president of the United States, please pay attention."

Ivins' wit inspired her audiences; she believed that fun, laughter, and passion were essentials for a well-lived life. She thrived on controversy and loved to be in the thick of it. Her two greatest honors were being banned from a Texas university campus and having a Minnesota police mascot pig named after her. She even bandied words with her stage III inflammatory breast cancer. "Having breast cancer is massive amounts of no fun. First they mutilate you, then they poison you, then they burn you. I have been on blind dates better than that." Ivins glowed with creative spirit. She sparkled with determination and fizzed with passion and courage. She taught others to live in the moment and laugh whenever possible.

American writer Hortense Calisher collected words for future creative sprees. She exclaimed, "The words! I collected them in all shapes and sizes and hung them like bangles in my mind." This type of inspiration is drawn to a vast spectrum of material; it is a foraging mastermind. It is the force behind writers collecting words and phrases, artists storing color samples, and chefs who cannot have too many utensils. Inspiration is the quartermaster who requisitions and the earth mother who dispenses. Like a comet, inspiration can leave trails of unfettered ingredients for the taking. "Live each moment as if your hair is on fire" recommends artist Suzannah B. Troy. I agree, but from experience I can tell you that sometimes the direct approach does not work, and a little subtlety is required.

The magic of inspiration can be elusive. It straddles fantasy and practicality, nimbly engaging unconscious associations and rearranging ideas. Always busy, but not always at our beck and call, its enchantment slips in and out of mesmerizing possibilities. We cannot always summon inspiration on the first attempt. Sometimes daydreaming and meditating stimulate the magic lamp of creative inspiration, releasing genie-dusted impressions. Quiet, unscheduled blocks of time charm inspiration to materialize where we need the magic most.

Stepping back and doing something else gives inspiration some breathing room. Activity not related to the particular problem under consideration can lure solutions, options, and insights out into the open. How many times have I been stuck on a crossword clue? How many times have I put it aside then picked it up later and immediately known the answer? I love the advice of Agatha Christie, one of my favorite English mystery writers, on subverting a missing inspirational muse. "The best time to write a book is while you're doing the dishes." Inspiration works like that.

Spirituality is powered from a source considered greater than self. Creative insight transcends the ordinary when enlightened by spiritual energy. Hand-in-hand, inspiration and spirituality rise above barriers and limitations. Together, they summon personal insight and translate inner yearnings. They free us from the cadence of the ordinary into awe-inspiring wonder, harmony, and balance.

Creativity smiled upon by spirituality moves us beyond time. It strengthens our relationship with the universe and explores the interconnectedness of humankind. American-born English novelist Susan Ertz gently touches upon the ethereal nature of creativity when she says, "Millions long for immortality who don't know what to do with themselves on a rainy Sunday afternoon." It is an intangible web of linkages that enwraps our deepest roots. Spirituality gives meaning to existence, the nature of reality, and the quality of life.

CURIOUS

The cure for boredom is curiosity. There is no cure for curiosity.
—Dorothy Parker, Algonquin Round Table diva

Be less curious about people and more curious about ideas.
—Marie Curie, Nobel Prize-winning French physicist

Where would creativity be without rubbernecking curiosity? Restless and on the prowl for new enterprises, curiosity is interested in answers, questions, uncertainties and, well, just about everything. It happily ventures into the unfamiliar and untested and dallies with fresh possibilities. Curiosity stimulates the unasked and ambushes the unexpected. Sparked by the desire to experiment and explore, curiosity deactivates fear of failure and bottom line focus. Curiosity is a ticklish itch that feels good to scratch.

Inquiry amused by creativity provides giggles of surprises. It delights in riddles and mysteries. Unknowns become speculation and research topics. Inquisitive doubts goad the hunt for clues, meaning, and resolution. Curiosity pursues excitement and energizes breaks with routine. Fresh perspectives and unforeseen resources give rise to unexplored associations. Curiosity provides tinder and spark for creative fire.

Some people think Pandora deserves her bad rap, but I do not agree. She is an iconic woman who followed her curiosity to look beyond the forbidden. Her controversial peek exemplifies creative interest, audacity, and ambition.

✑ Pandora ✍

Never born, she will always live.

Pandora, Greek Goddess from mythological times, was the first news-breaking investigative reporter. Humanity's understanding of the world deepened as a result of her undaunted curiosity. Boldly ignoring the rules, Pandora's spunky drive and keen intellect spurred her to open the forbidden box.

Single-handedly, Pandora brought to light the human qualities of wrestling with problems and of feeling hope.

Her curiosity-fueled courage demonstrated a way to live life to the fullest.

—From Greek Mythology

I like to think of hers as a story about a courageous, inquisitive woman rather than a locked box. In Pandora's adventure, her curiosity is an asset that supports her as she moves beyond the forbidden to reveal what was once concealed. Curiosity has a way of fostering awareness by urging us to probe, examine, and test limits. It prowls around, ferreting out imaginative ideas. Curiosity scrutinizes incompatible concepts and sees fresh associations. It turns fantasy into reality, problems into solutions, and questions into answers.

Ah, Mae Jemison! She must have a curious soul. Dr. Jemison's curiosity took her on a journey far beyond Planet Earth. As a chemical engineer, scientist, physician, teacher, and astronaut, she accomplished a lot in the first half of her life. In 1992, Jemison, one of the first female astronauts, blasted into outer space on the Endeavor. As a science mission specialist, her onboard mission was to conduct experiments to research an absence of gravity's effect on living organisms. Looking down from Endeavor, Jemison said, "I felt like I belonged right there in space. I realized I would feel comfortable anywhere in the universe because I belonged to and was a part of it, as much as any star, planet, asteroid, comet, or nebula." When we encounter other life in the universe, I hope Mae Jemison, spirited space adventurer, is there to greet them.

Whether venturing into space at warp drive or moving at a gravity-controlled pace on terra firma, we are surrounded by intriguing, creativity-provoking resources. The universe is a treasure trove of raw material. Each of us devises our own map with a unique X marking the spot. Digging into shifting sands of skills, information, ideas, and experiences, we uncover creative loot. English author Dorothy Richardson got it right when she said, "Life is creation; self and circumstances the raw material."

I'm reminded now of Pam, a wild woman I interviewed for this book. Growing up in rural Minnesota, Pam's exposure to art was minimal. Her family valued her talent and encouraged her artistic pursuits. Pam remembers a time when she created a collage for her mother. Everyone in the family loved it. The artwork was immediately framed. "You could sell your work!" Their praise remains an ever-remembered morale booster. Pam continues to prove them right.

✑ Finding Stuff ✑

An interview with a wild woman

Pam is a real deal, wild woman artist. With acute aesthetic vision, she sees beauty and potential in a surprising assortment of objects. Resourcefulness and acquisition are powerful colors on her palette. Collected wires, nails, feathers, and fabrics become exquisite creations in her skilled hands. Pam transforms ordinary into extraordinary, giving new life and meaning to the old and no-longer-needed.

Pam relies on her collection of found objects. Looking for the unexpected captures the spirit of creative karma. Curiosity's provocative sidekick—serendipity—sparks breakthroughs by accidentally bumping into chance remarks and tripping over stray bits of information. Nothing we intentionally search for is found serendipitously. When creativity's wild child comes acallin', you just never know what will turn up.

Creativity's messy, random, and unpredictable nature has an affinity for flirty curiosity and serendipity. Follow-the-trail curiosity and sniff-the-roses serendipity have great affection for creativity.

RESOURCEFUL

This has been a most wonderful evening. Gertrude has said things tonight it will take her ten years to understand.
Alice B. Toklas, American literary icon

Existence is a party. You join after it's started and you leave before it's finished.
Elsa Maxwell, columnist, songwriter, professional host

Resourceful creativity likes the challenge of banishing the boring and taming the threatening. Creativity delights in provocation and is tickled pink to come up with outrageous choices and nimble responses. It is open to new experience, copes with diversity, and is comfortable with chaos. Creativity effectively reinterprets and refreshes experiences and insights. Resourceful adeptness sharpens the clout of originality and innovation.

Eleanor of Aquitaine, medieval queen of England, knew some creatively crafty ways around threats, challenges, and imprisonment. I have been fascinated by Eleanor since high school and now see her as a personification of creative resourcefulness. She was intelligent, rich, beautiful, and larger-than-life. Ingeniously, she took the imperfect and molded it into part of her plan to achieve her goals. For example, in medieval times women were not allowed to do much foreign traveling, but Eleanor, at the time she was queen of France, went to Syria on one of the Crusades. Eleanor of Aquitaine, played by Katharine Hepburn in *The Lion in Winter,* says, "I even made poor Louis take me on a Crusade. How's that for blasphemy? I dressed my maids as Amazons and rode bare-breasted halfway to Damascus. Louis had a seizure and I damn near died of windburn ... but the troops were dazzled."

Do not corner a resourceful woman, especially if she can outsmart or out wait you. Sometime later in life and after the crusade trip, Eleanor refused to give King Henry of England, her second husband, power over her land. She wanted to keep it for herself and later for her favorite son. Henry retaliated by locking her in prison. Eleanor turned this into a contest of wills by thriving in isolation and plotting with all three of their sons to usurp Henry's crown and kingdom. Eleanor's survival and release became a strategic game. Resourceful creativity at work!

One more Eleanor story: Eleanor outlived Henry and went on to create a court that centered on a culture of respect for women, children, and a theme of *make love, not war.* She traveled constantly, spreading and maintaining loyalty for England, negotiating and cementing marriage alliances for her grandchildren, and managing armies and estates. She lived into her eighties, wielding great financial and political power. Eleanor, as channeled by Hepburn, says, "As queen of England what would you have me do? Give out? Give up? Give in?"

Eleanor spoke with a voice of resourceful creativity and lived through adversity with panache. Perhaps this iconic queen would agree with Marlene Dietrich. In *Destry Rides Again*, Dietrich warbled in her inimitable voice, "See what the boys in the back room will have, and tell them that I'll have the same."

Inspired, curious, and resourceful women carry the creative feminine within. Spirited creative expression animates life with ever-rejuvenated energy. Women sense that creativity is a part of their nature and an extension of being female. They use creativity to adjust goals, reinvent dreams, reaffirm commitment, revive enthusiasm, and energize momentum. English prima ballerina Margot Fonteyn was *en pointe* when she said, "Generally speaking, we are all happier when we are still striving for achievement than when the prize is in our hands." I would like to add that, for me, creativity is a spritz of champagne. It improves life, uplifts spirits, and cures just about anything.

Chapter Two

Women: Nature & Nurture

If I were born once again, I would like to be a woman—always!

—Dame Agatha Christie, British mystery writer

I feel there is something unexplored about a woman that only a woman can explore.

—Georgia O'Keeffe, American artist

*L*et me confess right now that I have a passion for creativity, women, and women's ways of embracing the creative feminine. The mystique of women's creativity resonates with the collaborative spirit of nature and nurture and sings in harmony with the rhythms of mind and body. Just tune into the awesome force of the cycle from menarche to menopause and beyond, as it moves to a tempo of fun, exhilaration, and serious whimsy.

I remember falling in love with Nora Charles while watching *The Thin Man*, a 1934 classic comedy-mystery movie. The theater darkened, the credits played, and black and white images flickered on the screen. Nora and Nick, her detective husband, swoop through the film with playful energy and snappy repartee. Oh, to be Nora Charles, to understand and value the messiness of creating a life where the whimsical feminine presides. I loved the glamour, humor, and unabashedly flirtatious marriage and never truly surfaced from my voyeuristic plunge into Nora's wacky celebration of life.

✑ Nora Charles ✑

Never born, she will always live.

Nora Charles is witty, beautiful, and independently wealthy. As the self-confident, equal partner to her mystery-solving husband, Nora collects clues and helps solve crime. She is always game and ready to trap the murderer. Once, she threw herself in front of a crazed killer as he pointed a gun at Nick.

Nora lives life with humor. Her style is totally tongue-in-cheek class. Her response to the endless stream of race track touts, ex-cons, punch drunk wrestlers, and men with names like Fingers and Creeps: "Oh Nick, you know such interesting people." Nick describes her as a "lanky brunette with a wicked jaw." He is totally gone on Nora.

—*The Thin Man* 1934 movie based on Dashiell Hammett's 1934 novel

Together, Nick and Nora epitomize creative perspective. Life is how they see it. They like what they see and are prepared to enjoy whatever comes their way.

I enjoy my own creative perspective, centered on the creative process—even the hard work of it—because it is an ever expanding, on-the-move target. There is nothing better than hitting the bull's-eye or, better yet, missing and striking a surprise. I started to write a very serious book about women's development and how myriad paths lead us to become who we want to be. My creative feminine executed a screwball somersault; whimsy, humor, and celebration took over. But the underlying bedrock of the book I thought I would write (and the one you are reading now) is my admiration for women. Truly creative women convert wishing and hoping into connecting, learning, achieving, leading and, ultimately, presiding. Creative women transform actions into satisfying participation in life.

"While we have the gift of life, it seems to me the only tragedy is to allow part of us to die; whether it is our spirit, our creativity, or our glorious uniqueness." Comedian and actor Gilda Radner said that, and I agree with her. When I see the creative synergy of women's nature and nurture at work, I percolate with possibility. When I feel joyous, uplifted, energetic, and most like myself, I know my creative feminine is up to something.

As I spend more time focusing on women, I realize we all have a creative bent. Sometimes it just takes catching a glimpse from the right angle to see it in action. I am fascinated by the endless manifestations of women's power to be creative and struck by their inspiring and invigorating passion to create. The more aware I become of women's unique slant on creative endeavors, the more I see and appreciate.

Women's creative endeavors often gleam with brilliance, strength, humor, intuition, and courage. One of my university students, Sasha, chose Tippy, her Chihuahua, as the subject for the semester-long biography project. Sasha applied the concepts and assessments we studied to build Tippy's profile. Tippy was no stranger; she occasionally attended class, fashionably clad and snuggled in her color-coordinated carryall. The personal data and the interview were crafted to fit a canine point of view. One conclusion was Tippy was an extrovert. She loved going to the dog park to play and make new friends. In the process of creating the perfectly executed project, Sasha demonstrated brilliant understanding of concepts and an intuitive sense that I would get it. Grading her project was a hoot.

Women like Nora, Gilda, and Sasha blend experience and expectation to concoct lively enterprise. When in touch with their creative muses, women are not bound by rules, and they thrive on the excitement of finding and making new concoctions. Their minds and bodies are simpatico, and the power of nature and nurture is humming. Women high on creative whimsy are pretty darn exciting to be with, and they are highly contagious.

WELL-CONNECTED BRAINS

The truth will set you free. But first, it will piss you off.
Gloria Steinem, feminist, journalist

When I started working on women's history about thirty years ago, the field did not exist.
Gerda Lerner, historian, author, teacher

In the dark ages of neuroscience, brain functioning had to be inferred from behavioral or autopsied information, and it was assumed that women, including their brains, were small men except for differences related to reproduction. Technology has advanced, and brains at work can be studied in real time. Stumbling blocks are dwindling as scientific information increases.

Women have probably always known the physical power of their brains. Poet Emily Dickenson said, "If I feel physically as if the top of my head were taken off, I know that is poetry." Dickenson knew from experience that creative energy germinates in the folds of a lyrical brain. The English feminist essayist Virginia Woolf once recounted the effects of high-speed synaptic communication. She puzzled, "My own brain is to me the most unaccountable of machinery—always buzzing, humming, soaring, roaring, diving, and why? What's this passion for?" I bow to these early brain researchers.

A woman's brain is a perfect laboratory for creativity. Female brains are densely packed with neuronal fibers in the forward part of the corpus callosum, the lively link between cerebral hemispheres. The power-concentrated corpus callosum connects extensive and intricate interbrain communication that is nourished by blood flow between the brain's lobes. Women's ultra-facilitated hemispheric interface propels swift integration of information, detail, nuance, and memory and revs up verbal abilities.

These enhanced verbal and memory brain sites influence women's language fluency and linguistic proclivity. Women use close to 20,000 words a day. Women are rich storehouses of variegated aesthetic and emotional impressions. They tend to remember the spoken word, emotional events, and the minutest details.

The characteristics of female brain circuitry impact women's creative expression and surely carry weight with the goddess of the creative feminine. The skills that emerge from these proclivities influence women's approaches to creativity, relationships, learning, achieving, and leading, as well as developing and nurturing women's relationships with their personal creative side. Cindy has some great nature-bestowed, wild women circuitry. Friendly, observant, and detail-oriented, she nurtures her creative muse and tunes into her customers as they share their creative visions.

ᔕ Some Enchanted Gallery ᔕ

An interview with a wild woman

After raising three boys, Cindy was ready for a new challenge. As chance would have it, she went into a picture-framing gallery, was intrigued by what she saw, and was hired. Cindy now has a gallery of her own. With a spirit of adventure and a determination to transform clients' words and raw materials into artistic reality, she listens attentively and remembers both the basics and the subtler fine points. Cindy envisons their creative needs and uses her talent to make them a reality.

Cindy has framed many pictures for me. In each case, the framing was exactly what I had in mind, or better.

Cindy says, "I added just a tiny outline of gold around the mat. It needed something, so I thought this would add a subtle gleam." Her creative eye adds creative synergy to every project.

Cindy's well-connected brain has built a thriving business. As she chitchats with customers, she tunes in to detail and nuance. Cindy turns vision into finished product using the subjective information she attains through listening and remembering.

INTUITIVE BRAINS

Intuition comes very close to clairvoyance; it appears to be the extrasensory perception of reality.
Alexis Carrel, Nobel Prize laureate in physiology and medicine

Trust your hunches. They're usually based on facts just below the conscious level.
Dr. Joyce Brothers, psychologist, author

Intuition is woman's country. The female brain is wired for mental leaps, and synaptic speed is the heartbeat of women's intuitive insight. Almost simultaneously, the female brain can grasp the big picture and its parts in rapid left-brain, right-brain exchanges. This is most clearly demonstrated in women's enhanced communication of emotions and the much-lauded ability to perform multiple tasks concurrently.

Born in the brain and nourished by contextual information, intuition is a powerful voice that calls for a heedful ear. Academy Award-winning actor Ingrid Bergman advised, "You must train your intuition. You must trust the small voice inside you which tells you exactly what to say, what to decide." Female brains register gut feelings with alacrity. Creative women have a predilection for context. Connections and intuition underlie the creative drive for unique approaches to choice, growth, and success.

More than a guess or a hunch, intuition is an immediate knowing without logical, concrete references. The language of intuition extends beyond words and defies logical evaluation. The vibes of intuition are involuntary and spontaneous, evoking the previously unsuspected. Women's intuition is attuned to the body's internal communiqués. Twinges in the shoulders, prickles on the back of the neck, churning in the stomach, and racing hearts have meaning for intuition. Pam, my wild women artist friend, described her intuition as a nudge or a "needing to do." Heeding her intuition proved to be life-changing.

∽ Intuition Makes a House Call ∾

An interview with a wild woman

As Pam planned her birthday party, she kept feeling that she needed to invite Tom, but it kept slipping her mind. Some small but persistent internal jab continued to urge her to invite Tom. Pam's intuition relentlessly prompted, "Ah, go ahead." So she made the call. Tom came and brought a friend. In getting acquainted with the friend, Pam was told of a house for sale. She ended up buying that very house. Her intuition was on the mark.

Women are uniquely connected to creativity when they tap their intuitive powers. As an artist, Pam respects her instincts, encourages them to nurture her creative inspirations, and successfully manifests her intuitive visions.

Women's intuition stimulates perceptions that spring from nuance, detail, and emotion. Anthropologist and social critic Margaret Mead explained women's distinctive style of intuition in saying, "Because of their age-long training in human relations—for that is what feminine intuition really is—women have a special contribution to make to any group enterprise." Spontaneous and nonlinear intuition winkles out unrelated facts and ideas and captures salient solutions.

The high octane affiliation between women and intuition is legendary. Women's brains are built to notice, interpret, and remember nonverbal information. They take in posture, gesture, expression and voice. Agatha Christie's amateur detective, Jane Marple, relies on her intuition to interpret village life and catch murderers. Whether gossiping over the fence or casually conversing, Marple gathers information and impressions that lead to untangled mysteries.

✍ Jane Marple ✎

Never born, she will always live.

Jane Marple appears to be an ordinary, slightly ditzy old lady who likes knitting fluffy stuff. However, in her fictional reality, she is steel-trap sharp, shrewd, and intuitive. In addition to gardening and knitting, she loves to solve murders and does not shrink from viewing the body. Miss Marple perpetually embarrasses the plodding professionals by solving murders that have them scratching their heads.

What is the secret of her success? Jane Marple's results are fueled by offhand remarks, hawk-eyed observation, and spot-on intuition. She knows that context is a shrewd messenger loaded with information. Miss Marple accurately appraises the patterns of human behavior exhibited in St. Mary Mead, her sleepy microcosm of the world. Marple's well-stocked intuition makes the essential connection, "The murderer reminds me of little Tommy Brown who always . . . ." She unerringly identifies the murderer and explains the mystery.

—Agatha Christie's sleuth first introduced in the 1930 novel *The Murder at the Vicarage*

Though fictional, Marple is a good example of intuitively creative women. She fashions a most interesting, unconventional life built around her interests, hobbies, and talents. Confidently leaping from insight to inspiration, she rises above the puzzling, recalcitrant, or pedestrian, aglow with creative energy.

HOT CHROMOSOMES AND HORMONES

All my life, I always wanted to be somebody. Now I see that I should have been more specific.
Jane Wagner, writer, director

I am a woman; on this truth must be based all further discussion.
Simone de Beauvoir, French existentialist, writer, social essayist

Women's bodies are celebrations of creativity. Life sings with the rapture of our bodies' cycles and hums with the creative power of our hormones and chromosomes. Physical and mental rejuvenation require creative sustenance to escalate our adaptability. As a result, women have been outliving men for centuries. So why is that important to the creative process? Well, nature and nurture saturate us with the urge and the talent to create. Longevity imbues us with a sense of unfolding seasons and time. Working in cahoots, nature, nurture, and longevity provide abounding opportunities to develop and use our creativity. In a nutshell, long life means we have more time to work on it and get it right.

Women outlast men by about eight years. Female centenarians outnumber men nine to one. The reasons for the disparity in life expectancy are biological as well as behavioral. Genetics and hormones contribute to women's longevity, as do loads of cultural, social, and psychological factors. Women have a pair of X chromosomes, which seems to contribute to physiological endurance. This couplet means that women have less risk of suffering harmful consequences if an X chromosome has a defective gene. Women have a backup, duplicate X. It also provides a double dose of factors that regulate the immune system.

Until menopause, women have a hormonal edge against heart disease. Estrogen, a female sex hormone, can prevent or slow down heart disease. It has beneficial effects on cardiovascular health by decreasing the level of low-density fats and cholesterol in the bloodstream.

One hundred years ago the average life expectancy for women was forty-nine; today it is eighty. Women may live longer because of the way they deal with stress and threats. The release of oxytocin is a part of the stress response. This hormone buffers the fight-or-flight response and produces a tend-or-befriend response. The response encourages caring for children and gathering with other women. When engaged in tending and befriending, more oxytocin is released, further countering stress and producing a calming effect. American author Dorothy Parker wrote about the warmth of friendship, not knowing its role in women's longevity: "Constant use had not worn ragged the fabric of their friendship." Estrogen seems to enhance the effects of oxytocin. This sequence does not occur in men because of testosterone, which appears to reduce the effects of oxytocin.

Women's less confrontational response fosters the cultivation of social and emotional connection. A less in-your-face response lowers blood pressure and reduces the risk of heart disease, stroke, and death or injury from physical combat. English novelist Mary Ann Evans, better known as George Elliot, said, "I am not denyin' that women are foolish; God Almighty made 'em to match men." But fewer women are killed at work, on the streets, or by their own hands. Women are less often murdered. When they are, it is usually by men and not other women. Women are less likely to be employed in hazardous occupations, drive recklessly, start and fight wars, or go to prison.

From menarche to climacteric and beyond, with PMS, hot flashes, and orgasms in between, the female life cycle is a remarkable series of physical phenomena and passages. The accompanying hormonal shifts of puberty, menstruation, and menopause instigate hormonal-revved and endorphin-driven creativity. Diarist Anais Nin expressed the nature of growth and transition, saying, "There came a time when the risk to remain tight in the bud was more painful than the risk it took to blossom." Creativity shapes women's responses to nature-proffered physical crossroads and nurture-bestowed emotional transitions.

"When nothing is sure, everything is possible," English novelist Margaret Drabble captures the awesome possibilities of life. *When will my period start? Will I get married? How many children will I have?* These are just a few of the many questions we ponder. The aura surrounding women's bodies inspires awe and reverence, conjuring a sense of the unknown and unknowable. Menstruation, pregnancy, childbearing, motherhood, marriage, and menopause are not simply life-cycle events. They are institutions that carry socio-cultural legacies that do not occur in isolation.

Dramatic metamorphoses occur in adolescence. It is a time of maximum physical growth and a social-emotional transition from childhood to young adulthood. Menarche, or first menstruation, is a physical and social milestone indicating the body's coming readiness. It occurs during preteen or early teen years, with full reproductive powers and ovulation occurring several years later. The onset of puberty is a nexus of physical change filled with passionate intensity. Author Judy Blume touched on adolescent angst in this one-sided conversation. "It's me, Margaret. I just told my mother I want a bra. Please help me grow, God. You know where. I want to be like everyone else." Preteen girls enter puberty looking like children and, within four or five years, emerge young women. Mental and physical transformation transports girls into the power and responsibility of womanhood.

Accommodating puberty is not easy. Pop celebrity Britney Spears explained it this way: "I did not have implants; I just had a growth spurt." Adolescence is a time to try on many looks and identities. Enormous energy is expended in fitting the right image, striving for perfection, attending to others' expectations, and being unique. My wild woman colleague Harriet understands the challenge. Drawing on a doctorate in family therapy, here's what Harriet did for her two daughters.

∽ The Birthday Party ∾

An interview with a wild woman

Harriet created a special event—a "Coming into Womanhood Party." Invitations were sent, scrumptious food was prepared, and champagne corks popped. Harriet invited her close female friends, and each came ready to share their personal take on being a woman.

Harriet wanted her daughters to hear about women from women, not just girlfriends, boyfriends, or the media. Each woman brought a special token of significance; the gifts and stories were shared with Harriet's daughters. One friend brought a cutting from a rose bush that had originated in her grandmother's garden.

Both of Harriet's daughters balked at first, but afterward they expressed how moved they were by the women's stories. Leslie and Katherine still talk about their parties.

Ask Harriet about her greatest accomplishment, and she will say it is raising her daughters. She delights in their confidence, strengths, capabilities, and choices. It does not always unfold that way for adolescent girls. Novelist Barbara Kingsolver described this doubt and unease when she wrote about the vulnerability of girls: "Why is it that only girls stand on the sides of their feet? As if they're afraid to plant themselves?"

Historically culture suggested that girls act demurely and sub-due their liveliness. The present demands a broader view of young women that extends beyond the realm of giggling about boys and shopping. Today's young women develop the desire to nurture their capacity to live and feel fully and to be the authority in their own lives. Current thinking allows young women to discover to what depths they will embrace or reject life's choices.

Menstruation is a monthly surge of hormonal zingers. Actor Cybill Shepherd quipped, "It's okay to talk about birth, okay—then menstruation. I first started my advocacy for women's health in the field of reproductive freedom, and the next stage would be bringing menopause out of the closet." Tied to the ebb and flow of fertility the repetitive cycle signifies youth, health, and plumbing in good working order.

Cultural taboos and lack of information complicate an event that indicates a functioning reproductive system. In the past, menstruating women were isolated, prohibited from participat-ing in sports, and excluded from anything that might require clear thinking. As a culture, we continue to think of menstruation as a hygiene problem and an embarrassing event better kept under wraps. A woman experiences about 400 monthly periods, encom-passing about half of her life. In some cultures, menstrual blood is believed to have magical and healing powers. It is said to purify, cleanse, and renew. Some women report that they feel more cre-ative, artistic, and insightful during their periods.

Not a disorder, menopause is a period of physical and emotional change. Culture's perception of mid-life women and aging is steeped in the value placed on fertility, youth, and beauty. Anthropologist Margaret Mead said succinctly, "There is no more creative force in the world than the menopausal woman with zest." We now know that as women mature and develop, their creativity blossoms, enlarging and deepening their contributions and expectations.

Menopause is no longer a secret. It has been outed and can be talked about. Women now take responsibility for this stage of development, seeing its place in the cycle of life. By gathering current information and banishing outdated perceptions, each woman constructs personal meaning, incorporating her freedoms and frustrations. Announcing a second adulthood, menopause conjures new aspects of femininity.

Contemporary women have the power to plan their futures acknowledging and welcoming strengths, self-worth, and wisdom. This approach to mid-life ameliorates its cloud of loss and finality. Germaine Greer, author and feminist diva, hit the nail on the head: "Though there is no rite of passage for women approaching the end of her reproductive years, there is evidence that women devise their own ways of marking the irrevocability of the change. Menopause is a time of taking stock, of spiritual as well as physical change, and it would be a pity to be unconscious of it."

Women live an average of thirty years beyond menopause. Survival beyond fertility suggests women are necessary to the species even when no longer able to bear children. Embrace these years as a time for reflection, discoveries, actions, and dreams. Post-menopausal women are the repositories of wisdom, information, and skill. They give fresh meanings to maturity. Take the advice of Isadora Duncan, mother of modern dance: "You were once wild here. Don't let them tame you." Creative energy is like springtime, always ready to return, renewed and refreshed after a long series of life events.

Two Hollywood legends share wise women perspectives on the longevity issue. Bette Davis offered bald truth, "Old age is no place for sissies." Sophia Loren's perspective is lyrical, "There is a fountain of youth: it is your mind, your talents, the creativity you bring to your life, and the people you love. When you learn to tap this source, you have truly defeated age."

COOL CHOICES

All the strength you need to achieve anything is within you. Don't wait for a light to appear at the end of the tunnel. Stride down and light the bloody thing yourself.
Sarah Henderson, Australian cattle woman

It is easy to follow, but it is uninteresting to do easy things. We find out about ourselves only when we take risks, when we challenge and question.
Magdalena Abakanowicz, Polish sculptor

Women are the presiding geniuses of their fascinating lives! Wild-women resourcefulness and insight enhance self-determination and decision making. Our choices related to marriage, motherhood, self-care, and aging are everyday proof of our creative nature.

We have influenced cultural changes and embraced the rewards of our efforts. Women continue to transform limited options into kaleidoscopic worlds of expanded possibilities.

In *Toward a New Psychology of Women*, Jean Baker Miller detailed women's distinctive ways of interacting with the world. Written in 1976, this landmark book underscored the positive effects of women's relational, cooperative, and interpersonal strengths. Miller's thoughtful work expanded our thinking about the importance of women's creativity, energy, and courage. She underscored women's responses to creativity's many invitations to revel in our powers to grow, change, and make things better. Diane Mariechild's artful insight reiterated this uniquely female way of being. She wrote, "A woman is the full circle. Within her is the power to create, nurture and transform. A woman knows that nothing can come to fruition without light. Let us call upon woman's voice and woman's heart to guide us in this age of planetary transformation."

Unexamined assumptions, expectations, and attitudes can conceal stereotypic restrictions and barriers. Sharp-witted women of vision know this. Time and time again they question the status quo and develop broader circles of influence. More importantly, women have self-reflective grit. They are willing to delve into their thoughts and beliefs and reevaluate. Bringing into play all of their wit and wisdom, women shape futures.

To be or not to be a wife? A mother? Nowadays these two questions have morphed into an alternative-enriched selection. Thanks to enlightened social-cultural expectations, women's choices have expanded. Take a peek with me.

Not that long ago marriage and motherhood—always in that sequence—were the feminine ideal. Women have since discovered that they do not need marriage or children, in any order or combination, to be complete, fulfilled, or in touch with the creative feminine. What is truly awesome is that marriage and motherhood are still going strong.

Motherhood and mothering are wonderful adventures, but that path is not for every woman. The reality of mothering has been romanticized and idealized. It is a fulfilling challenge, potentially enjoyable, hard work, and never completed. Being a mother can be exciting and emotionally stimulating, bringing great responsibility and satisfaction, as well as a little stress. Nina Paley, artist, cartoonist, and filmmaker, put a humorous spin on this serious undertaking. "Choosing to have children is like choosing to play the bagpipes: you must do it well or not at all. Anything in between and you'll really annoy your neighbors."

Author Elizabeth Stone imparted the deep tenderness that motherhood can evoke: "Making the decision to have a child—its momentous. It is to decide forever to have your heart go walking around outside your body." I understood this quote intellectually but it was not until Jagger, my six-year-old nephew, came to live with me after a hurricane evacuation that my heart fully comprehended. When he was able to return to his family, a part of me went forever with him.

Only women have the biological power to give life and have babies. Whether conception takes place by choice or chance, childbearing preference is influenced by deeply held values and beliefs and is shaped by cultural expectations. Some women choose to be single parents, some choose a childfree life. Options. Choices. Decisions. Relationships with partner, parents, family, and friends impact all three. Actress Margot Bennett stated, "As time passes, we all get better at blazing a trail through the thicket of advice."

Being unmarried is not catastrophic. There is no single-woman taboo. Single life can be a choice. Marrying later, divorcing more, and outliving their husbands, single women are unquestionably a major force in our culture. "One person's constant is another person's variable," professes Dr. Susan Gerhart, university professor. She could be philosophizing about marriage: yes, no, maybe, again, or forget about it. Womanhood, marriage, and motherhood are no longer tied in one inevitable bundle. This change has enriched the scope of women's lives and broadened their opportunities to invest their creativity.

Widows, abandoned or divorced women, women with disabled or sick husbands—single women have always been a part of our culture. They take care of themselves, their children, and many others. I am inspired by the philosophy of Impressionist painter Mary Cassatt: "I am independent! I can live alone and I love to work." Women as helpless and fragile? No way.

In the past, marriage and family were thought to be the best arenas for women's creative energy and talent. With creative capacity unfurled, women move beyond traditional parameters and conventional expectations and enrich the scope of the world. Nancy Goodman Brinker is an admirable example of female effectiveness and influence at work in a world-encompassing venue.

She supercharged her nurturing instincts with a blast of focused business acumen. In 1982, Brinker made a promise. As her sister, Susan Goodman Komen, was dying of breast cancer, Nancy vowed to do all that she could to find a cure for this devastating disease. The inauguration of The Race for the Cure was the means to that end. This national, grassroots movement raises millions of dollars to support advocacy, build awareness, and fund research. For 25 years Brinker has inspired women to battle for progress in the fight to defeat cancer. The mission of the now named Susan G. Komen for the Cure is to totally eradicate breast cancer. Activist and author Marion Wright Edelman summarizes the idea: "Who ever said anybody has the right to give up?"

Call it aging, maturing, mellowing, graying, or getting old—the process still beats the alternative. In her unique and unorthodox style, Muriel Spark had her stand-against-convention-hero Miss Jean Brody state, "Be on the alert to recognize your prime at whatever time of life it may occur." That is an approach I can go with. Have you noticed that what may be skeptically received from a young woman will get applauded when it comes from an older woman? Three cheers for prime.

The structure of our time on earth is pretty well set: birth, life and death; past, present, and future. Unfolding in steps, spirals, leaps, and dips, we move through life in cycles of accomplishment, loss, challenge, and persistence. Time, we discover, only exists today. And as Carrie Fisher, Princess Leia's alter ego, said, "Instant gratification takes too long." Ah, but here is the good news. Within the intersections of life and time, creativity comes into its own.

Tomorrow evolves from today, presenting the feminine creative with innumerable invitations.

With extended life expectancy, achieving milestones has become less regimented and more fluid. Becoming an adult begins earlier and extends well into the ninth decade. We can grow old without being fossilized. If we did not quite get it the first time around, chances are we'll get another shot. This may be my favorite sassy take on aging crafted as only Alice Babette Toklas could: "Haven't you learned yet that it isn't age but lack of experience that makes us fall off ladders or have radiators fall on us?"

We are all affected by life-extending science and life-enhancing technology. Current medical discoveries and technological inventions radically reshape daily life and human options. Here is a tip straight from Florida Scott-Maxwell, playwright and Jungian analyst, to seniors everywhere who like to dance. "My kitchen floor is so black and shiny that I waltz while I wait for the kettle to boil. This pleasure is for the old who live alone." Long life is here to stay, and growing old is inevitable. Yet even so, life is a cliffhanger. Aging brings new opportunities and outlooks. We create the variations and options.

Women, on average, have an eight-year longevity advantage. Some of it is the female chromosome and hormone invigorator, and some of it is the gift of inherited genetic material. Another piece of the almost decade-long boon is the interest women take in their own health. They will typically see a doctor for an ailment, prompting early diagnosis and more successful treatment. Women usually follow and complete a course of treatment. They tend to smoke and drink less than men. Here is some advice on choosing a doctor from Canadian actor Sarah Chalke: "What doctor does not need platform heels and dark black eyeliner to treat patients?"

The chimera of old age is routed by creative shenanigans. Learning to play and making younger friends add more to life's enjoyment than retirement income. So start now, begin today. Make friends, have fun, and stay young at heart. Remember the wise words of writer and director Jane Wagner: "A sobering thought: What if, at this very moment, I am living up to my potential?" Rena, a groundbreaking journalist and bestselling author, keeps her potential hopping. She is a wild word-woman who stays way ahead of old age by keeping close to her creative feminine. In this side story, she speaks of her creative kookiness.

✑ **Footnote** ✑

An interview with a wild woman

Rena introduced me to the age-old art of tattooing. Tattoos have been around since Cro-magnon times. Recently the slightly tarnished reputation of the tattoo has been rehabilitated, and its popularity has made a mainstream comeback. Rena explained that tattoos are expressions of personal meaning and always have a story.

Of course, Rena has a tattoo. Hers is a tiny musical note located on the front of her left ankle. The rousing foot note pays homage to her do-it-my-way style. This carefully chosen symbol translates her love of music into playfully creative humor.

From time to time I contemplate getting a tiny star or crescent moon tattooed on my wrist bone. I am just not there yet, Rena. Maybe someday I will indulge my sense of whimsy.

Jeanne Louise Calment, Frenchwoman extraordinaire, attributed her long life to wine, laughter, and olive oil. She rode her bike until she was one hundred and took up fencing at eighty-five. She didn't give up chocolate or smoking until she was 119. "I've never had but one wrinkle, and I'm sitting on it." She remained witty and alert until her death.

At 122 years and 164 days, Calment posthumously holds the title for longest confirmed lifespan. Researchers believe her longevity was related to her ability to rebuff stress. She said, "If you can't do anything about it, don't worry about it." Jeanne Louise was surely a sister-in-spirit with Lillian Carter. At age eighty-five, this nurse, Peace Corps volunteer, and former presidential mother said, "Sure, I'm for helping the elderly. I'm going to be old myself some day."

As someone who intends to live long, age gracefully, and wring every ticking second of my life for all it is worth, I am studying this aging issue closely. You can bet that creativity is going to be my anti-aging elixir of choice. Let me share a brief sampling of some of my favorite bits of wisdom from notable women.

Sometimes we become so entangled in the mundane facts of our lives that we forget about our creative nature until it starts nagging us with reminders of its needs or until we feel so fractured we know something is wrong.
Anne Hazard Aldrich, American author

Life is change. Growth is optional. Choose wisely.
Karen Kaiser Clark, lecturer, consultant, educator, author

Total absence of humor renders life impossible.
Sidonie Gabrielle Colette, French novelist

Almost anything is easier to get into than out of.
Agnes Allen, author

Without sustaining interests, connections, and curiosity, old age sucks. Somebody asked me if women grow old more gracefully. I said yes, indeed they can and do. Zelda Sayre Fitzgerald, American artist and quintessential southern belle, stated with elegance that she "refused to be bored chiefly because she wasn't boring." This is my plan for exquisitely mellowing into ageless grace. Live each day with at least a soupcon of creativity and be ready to take adventurous journeys. Weave youthfulness into my thoughts and actions. Be willing to flow beyond arbitrary, outmoded limits and stereotypic views. Stay close to those I love and risk being true to my creative passion.

Chapter Three

Women: History & Culture

*I think about how much we owe to the women who went before us-
legions of women, some known but many more unknown. I applaud the
bravery and resilience of those who helped all of us—you and me—to be
here today.*

—Ruth Bader Ginsburg, Supreme Court Justice

A hundred years from now? All new people.

—Anne Lamott, author, dotcom columnist

Yes, yes, yes, women influence history and culture, and within the whirlpools of culture and history, the feminine creative spirit flourishes. We are all aswim in the greatness of history and culture.

HISTORY TELLS STORIES

Remember our heritage is our power; we can know ourselves and our capacities by seeing that other women have been strong.
Judy Chicago, feminist artist

Remember, Ginger Rogers did everything Fred Astaire did, but backwards and in high heels.
Faith Ryan Whittlesley, former U.S. ambassador to Switzerland

History keeps us posted. Women's lives, work, passion, and social vision are a part of history. As shareholders in humanity, our stories and contributions are essential. Women's contributions were officially noticed in 1987 when Congress approved a resolution declaring March as National Women's History Month. Some might say, "Too little, too late." I say history is about acknowledging the past and influencing the future.

Women make up half of humankind and have always been crucial contributors in history. Our expertise and strength shape the world we share with men. Women's perspectives and contributions are essential and enrich the story. Exclusion or minimization of one-half of the population narrows the vision for all. So by ignoring the influential role of women, it becomes easier to perpetuate the myth that women are less strong, enlightened, dedicated, and vocal. Not a good idea.

History, after all, is creative fiction, with selections, deletions, and interpretations driven by writers and winners. The unfolding sagas that form the past are not immutable, but are ever-changing and socially constructed. Novelist Paula Gunn Allen wrote, "I have noticed that as soon as you have soldiers, the story is called history. Before their arrival, it is called myth, folklore, legend, fairy tale, oral poetry, ethnology. After soldiers arrive, it is called history." Generally, women were not invited or allowed to be agents in the construction or telling of history. Their points of view went unsolicited, voices were muffled, and women's stories were virtually ignored by historians. But history is more than waging war. History is the story of humanity.

Women look to past generations to gain perspective. Figures that inhabit bygone eras emerge as archetypes, and overlapping generations become accomplices in the preservation of humanity's story. Women definitely made history and influenced humanity. In the sixth century, the beguiling actress Theodora captured the heart of Byzantium's emperor. When Justinian and Theodora married, she became empress. As a powerful woman in a time and culture that considered women weak, Theodora used her influence, intellect, and political savvy to expand women's rights to the full extent accorded men. At any point in time, we are capable of radical individualism and revolutionary acts.

Women's perspective is essential to historical integrity. Our views on relationships, family, education, work, politics, and most of all, equality have guided our actions and shaped our reality. Jill Ruckelshaus, United States government official and lecturer, described one perspective that all women have shared. She captured so much more than dancing when she bantered, "It occurred to me when I was thirteen and wearing white gloves and Mary Janes and going to dancing school, that no one should have to dance backward all of their lives." Joleen, a forward-looking community volunteer and leader, rarely dances backwards. Her outlook is contagiously enthusiastic, and she is often found at the center of a creative hullabaloo.

✑ Let's Go ✑

An interview with a wild woman

Joleen says, "Nurture those you love and reflect their creativity back to them." With practical logic, she translates the needs and interests of family, friends, and community into enriching opportunities for all. Joleen was in on the conceptualizing, planning, and organizing of a three-day, city-wide, women-in-leadership event. She never broke a sweat. When invited by her children, she has ventured into new worlds of computers, music, sailing, gymnastics, and operating an espresso machine.

One day, Joleen called me. "I'm a member of the state Leadership Association, a group of fantastically vital women. They're having an athenaeum in a couple of weeks. You would love it and would fit right in. We'll only be gone for a few days, so pack your bag. I will pick you up and we can drive together." Of course, I said, "I'm packing already!"

Joleen is a great role model. She exemplifies many of the ways that women affect history. Daughters, mothers, and wives influence families, communities, nations, and the world. Women's voices are crucial. Without the abounding creativity of women, current history would be unrecognizable.

Women's achievements and contributions have frequently been overlooked, dismissed, and undocumented. Nonetheless, women's creative accomplishments are evident in history's landscape. As mystery writer Martha Grimes sees it, "We don't know who we are until we see what we can do." In World War II, women became pilots, passing the same tests for ability, endurance, and safety that were used to assess male pilots. After the war, these same women were offered airline jobs as stewardesses. Woman's place in history is significant. In spite of omissions and constraints, women have transformed history with their talents.

Feminism

*I myself have never been able to find out precisely what femi-
nism is; I only know that people call me a feminist whenever I
express sentiments that differentiate me from a doormat.*
Rebecca West, English journalist, novelist

The human contribution is the essential ingredient.
Ethel Percy Andrus, American social activist

Much like creativity, feminism refuses to be constrained by a
single definition. We know female wisdom is a complex, heteroge-
neous ethos that addresses the social, cultural, and political inequities that discriminate against women. Looking at feminism from a
historical perspective gives us an overview of the issues and rights
that have been at the heart of woman's ever-evolving quests.

Feminism is a response to events and conditions. Rooted in the
view of women as competent and expert about themselves, it is a
way of thinking that considers women's lives important. Motivated
by the experiences of women and informed by an understanding
of women's perspectives, feminism resoundingly impacts the lives
of women. By tapping women's rich diversity of wisdom and talents, feminists broaden traditional ideas about women.

Creative zest animates feminism. It heightens awareness and
spurs the initiation of alternative institutions and tactics. Wonder
Woman was the first and still is the most famous female super-
hero. A true feminist, she inspires women to become strong and
independent and invites us to imagine and create a safer world.

✐ Wonder Woman ✎

Never born, she will always live.

Wonder Woman was born on Paradise Island, homeland of the immortal Amazon women. Starting life as Princess Diana, she is blessed with wisdom, strength, speed, and empathy. Her mission to the United States: spread the ideals of love, peace, and sexual equality.

As Diane Prince, she tends to those injured in the fight against evil. Rather than punishing criminals, she reforms them. When women's issues are at stake, she transforms into Wonder Woman with a few twirls and a quick flick of her lasso. Wonder Woman fights for rights in a brass bra, star-spangled shorts, and red high-heeled boots.

—Created by William Moulton Marston in 1941 for DC Comics

We all have a little Wonder Women in us. Heroic women clear paths toward women's rights; create support networks that change the world in positive, uplifting ways; and inspire women to improve the future. Feminists acknowledge, nurture, and put into service the contributions of women. Their commitments are to the full development of all women.

Feminism is one such network of wonder women, with a history of heroic women battling for women's rights and social development. Feminism, by its nature, respects differences; taps a diversity of beliefs, priorities, and strategies; and thrives on opposition and disagreement. Life's injustices often initiate daring and great-hearted endeavors. Two-time Olympic pentathlete Marilyn King attested from her own training, "If you can't imagine it, you can never do it. In my experience, the image always precedes the reality." Women gave birth to a creative outpouring of social transformation in feminism, and their creative spirits and abilities keep that viewpoint alive as an ongoing social force.

There is no synonym for feminist listed on Thesaurus.com, and Dictionary.com describes a feminist as one who supports feminism. I like the way feminist author Margaret Atwood put it. "Does feminist mean a large unpleasant person who'll shout at you or someone who believes women are human beings? To me it is the latter, so I sign up." Me, too! Feminists affirm women's capacities to be capable and successful.

The epic adventure story of the feminist movement, as written so far, unfolds in three chapters cleverly titled First Wave, Second Wave, and Third Wave. As one of the main characters, the creative feminine characterizes the motivating, rabble-rousing provocateur. Women made history, changed history, co-created the world of today.

First Wave

The Queen is most anxious to enlist everyone in checking this mad, wicked folly of 'Women's Rights.' It is a subject which makes the Queen so furious she cannot contain herself.
Queen Victoria, Queen of England, Empress of India

If particular care and attention is not paid to the ladies, we are determined to foment a rebellion, and will not hold ourselves bound by any law in which we have no voice or representation.
Abigail Adams, abolitionist, feminist

Fierce courage guided the founding mothers of the women's rights movement. Formed by a small group of visionary women on a campaign against inequity, early feminists worked for the rights of women to own property, vote, and be educated. They articulated the prerogative of women to have intellectual, economic, and political aspirations and expectations.

The successful passage of the New York Married Woman's Property Rights Act in 1848 generated the initial nucleus of feminist energy. Before this law was passed, upon marrying, women lost any right to control property that had been theirs before marriage and were denied the right to acquire any property during their marriages.

The first wave of feminist activity was inaugurated at the Seneca Falls Convention later that same year. Elizabeth Cady Stanton, a young wife and new mother, crafted the original Declaration of Sentiments. Working on the premise that all men and women were created equal, she listed the usurpations of women's rights and asserted the resolutions and actions needed to address those injustices. This document shaped women's vision of liberty. Passionate first wavers sought social, civil, religious, and economic rights for women and other disenfranchised groups. Suffragist Susan B. Anthony stated what was to become an enduring feminist battle cry. "Men, their rights and nothing more; women, their rights and nothing less."

First Wave mandates gave women opportunities to focus their creativity in new ways and in new arenas. Instead of only keeping home fires burning, clothes laundered, and families fed, now there were speeches to write, debates to win, and places to go. Author Judith Groch touched on the inspirational impetus of our first wave mothers' creative moxie when she wrote, "Those who have been required to memorize the world as it is will never create the world as it might be." Suffragists were engaged in broadening worlds, creating opportunities, and flexing creative muscle.

In 1850, Sojourner Truth's speech titled "Ain't I a Woman?" brilliantly communicated the creative essence of women's fight for equality. With artful wit she made a request. "If the first woman could turn the world upside down, then why not give women a chance to set it right?" Sojourner had the verbal prowess to deal with hecklers. When a man in the audience said her ideas did not amount to a fleabite, within a heartbeat she replied that if the Lord was willing, she would keep her challengers scratching.

Each suffragist invested her creative mind, mettle, and heart. They believed the right to vote, choose leaders, and make laws were essential freedoms and strove to comprehensively address women's access to equality. Contemporary poet Annie Dillard conveyed the creative spirit of these early freedom fighters. She reflected, "The dedicated life is worth living. You must give with your whole heart." Seventy-two years later, in 1920, women won the vote. At long last, freedom and inalienable rights expanded to include women.

Second Wave

I am my own woman.

Evita Peron, Argentinean feminist, political activist

Writing a humor column for Ms. Magazine always sounded like a punch line of a joke to me. That estimable publication tends toward the sober… Still, being female is often a comical proposition in this world, and being a Texas feminist is a particularly oxymoronic vocation."

Molly Ivins, author, political columnist, Texas feminist

The second wave of feminism hit shore in the activist-enriched 1960s and held creative sway through the '80s. The Commission on the Status of Women was established in 1961 to research conditions and recommend changes. The report documented discrimination against women in almost every arena of their lives.

Eleanor Roosevelt chaired the commission until her death in 1962. She declared, "The battle for the individual rights of women is one of long standing and none of us should countenance anything which undermines it."

Kishida Toshiko, a Japanese feminist, posed this provocative question: "If it is true that men are better than women because they are stronger, why aren't our sumo wrestlers in the government?" Women of this turbulent era found that leadership roles in traditional activism were blocked. So, creative second wavers formed their own organizations for equality and liberation rousing women to wield their power. Civil rights, equal employment, access to higher education, and legal access to contraception became political catalysts.

In 1963, Betty Friedan identified women's hunger for equal opportunity, fulfillment, and success. Her landmark book *The Feminine Mystique* captured women's yearnings to move beyond stereotypes. Freidan's spirited assertions about discrimination inspired women to find their own paths beyond the status quo. Big, bold, and tough, she reminded women that they have an obligation to respect and nurture their talents, minds, and ambitions and lay waste to discrimination.

The creative feminine's cachet got a boost during feminism's second wave. Women came together in a creative spirit of common cause, and the topic of women and women's studies became legitimate and of consequence. The solidarity that developed engendered a profound interest in women's history and gender issues. This phase influenced an emergence of creative thought and research into women's pasts, their roles in history, and their contributions to culture. In the mid 1990s, I was thrilled when I was asked to redevelop and teach a course on the psychology of women for The University of Texas at Dallas. I still remember how totally cool it felt to teach such a dynamite subject!

Third Wave

The presence of feminism in our lives is taken for granted. For our generation, feminism is like fluoride. We scarcely notice it—it's simply in the water.
Jennifer Baumgartner and Amy Richards, authors

Women are repeatedly accused of taking things personally. I cannot see any other honest way of taking them.
Marya Mannes, U.S. journalist, writer

Women of the third wave continue to tackle controversial and tough issues—issues that limit or oppress women: reproductive rights, affordable childcare, military service, religious leadership, domestic violence, and sexual harassment. Resourceful women are leading creative change in politics, arts, government, business, professions, sciences, trades, education, and religion.

Singer, songwriter, and third wave feminist icon Ani DiFranco thumbs her nose at convention. DiFranco founded her own record label, Righteous Babe Records, in the early 1990s. For more than a decade she toured in her Volkswagen, picking up gigs along the way. In 2002, her concert venue was Carnegie Hall. In her songs, DiFranco examines the effects that rape, violence, abortion, and sexism have on women's lives. She shares her thoughts about feminism. "My idea of feminism is self-determination, and it's very open-ended: every woman has the right to become herself and do whatever she needs to do."

Contemporary feminism incorporates history and past accomplishment with women's current needs. Some of the freedoms we currently experience are the result of the work, commitment, and creativity of previous generations. Feminists continue to work to provide women with their unalienable rights to fully participate in everyday life. They work so that women may govern, earn equal wages, play sports, and be published. They stand for equal opportunity, responsibility, and treatment based on talent and effort.

Present-day women capitalize on the personal freedoms realized by former generations in diverse, unpredictable, and original ways. Eve Ensler, author of *The Vagina Monologues* and *The Good Body*, is dedicated to stopping violence against women and making the world a place where women can thrive. Her words to the wise: "It seems to me that we spend an inordinate amount of time and attention on fixing ourselves when we could really be directing that out to serving others." Ensler chooses to serve others by writing plays about female body parts and the wonder of aging, imperfect female bodies. Her fine-tuned knack for touching our hearts can make you laugh and cry at the same time.

CULTURE PAINTS PICTURES

Contrary to popular opinion, Leave It to Beaver *was*
not a documentary.
Stephanie Coontz, author, educator

The true worth of a race must be measured by the character
of its womanhood.
Mary McLeod Bethune, educator, political activist

Culture sketches out life's set design. It has an ear for the storyline, enthusiasm for the players, and a talent for choreographing the future. Culture provides the color, detail, and vibe. It encompasses the creative style of the present, the tenor of the past, and the drift of creative endeavors to come. Eleanor Roosevelt, former first lady, vividly captured the cultural spirit of 1930s expectations for wives of important men. "Campaign behavior for wives: Always be on time. Do as little talking as humanly possible. Lean back in the parade car so everybody can see the president." Witness how much the roles of women in politics have changed.

Culture is as vast as an ocean and as busy as a hot tub on Saturday night. It shades the contours of life with values and beliefs impacting women and their complex and often paradoxical roles. Abruptly changing and fickle, culture provides powerful patterns for delineating boundaries, freedoms, and limitations.

Follow the cultural contradictions in this brief summary of work-related messages sent to women. During the Depression, women were discouraged from taking jobs so that men might have them. Once World War II was underway, women were encouraged to work and take the place of men so that they might fight. In the '50s, the golden rule was to stay home and be a housewife. The dictum in the '70s extolled the importance of building a career. Currently, we hear, "Do it all and find time for yourself." Martha Graham, modern dance pioneer, gently warns us, "There is only one of you in all time, this expression is unique. And if you block it, it will never exist through any other medium and it will be lost."

Cathy Drinkwater Better, journalist and poet, asserts our power to shape culture. "Life is raw material. We are artisans. We can sculpt our existence into something beautiful or debase it into ugliness. It's in our hands." Women and creativity frequently team to introduce new cultural directions and opportunities. French existentialist Simone de Beauvoir affirmed our capacity to develop our unique style. She says, "One is not born a woman, one becomes one." I say, take the bull by the horns and never avoid the wickedly fabulous prerogative of being in charge of your creative force.

Gender

Women share with men the need for personal success, even the taste for power, and no longer are willing to satisfy those needs through the achievement of surrogates, whether husbands, children or merely role models.
Elizabeth Dole, Republican senator from North Carolina

What are little girls made of?
sugar and spice,
and everything nice,
that's what little girls are made of.
Mother Goose, nursery rhyme

Now, take a minute and think. How do you feel about the old saying "girls will be girls"? What being female means, and how it is incorporated into behaviors, begins at birth. Parents set the process in motion by communicating their own and society's ideals. Gender-prescribed behavior is inherently part of educational, religious, and other cultural institutions. Culture overtly and covertly insinuates what it means to be female. For example, girls and women are expected to be verbal, caring, and nurturing, and we are still surprised when we find the opposite. Laurie Kuslansky noted, "Laugh and the world laughs with you. Cry and you cry with your girlfriends."

Gender-specific behavior is an intricate mix of biology and environment. There is overwhelming evidence that intellectual, emotional, and behavioral differences between males and females can be either promoted or de-emphasized. Gender often influences reactions and expectations. As Sylvia and I were yakking about career and family, I shared a bit about this book. Up until then I had only known her as a high-energy, mental health professional. That day she let me in on her wild-woman musician fame. She definitely thought this story fit the theme of the book. Here it is, Sylvia.

✑ **Drummer Girl** ✑

An interview with a wild woman

Sylvia, the most memorable drummer at St. Catherine's High School, talks about her musical talents with animation and pride. She was dynamite on the drums, not your typical girl instrument. Her mom was totally cool and supportive of Sylvia's wild-woman passions and percussions.

Different story at school. There she was mightily discouraged from trying out for the band. Drum playing was for boys. Sylvia practiced, persisted, and prevailed. St. Catherine's first girl drummer played with noisy enthusiasm and style.

Cultural presumptions influence women's visions of themselves and their options. What Sylvia experienced at school was not unique. Happily, she was able to stick with her ambitious plan supported by her mother's value for creative expression.

Courage, sensitivity, intellect, and, ultimately, creativity blast through cultural blinders.

Throughout history, women's gender roles have been defined by culture. Calamity Jane was a gal who knew how to broaden gender restrictions. In 1876, twenty-four-year-old Calamity Jane swaggered into Deadwood, South Dakota, wearing men's clothing. Pistol toting, chap-legged, and bandana-wrapped, she boasted that she could "out drink, out swear and out spit any man." Born Martha Jane Canary, she acquired her nickname by warning men they would be "courting calamity" if they offended her. Sharp-shooting, sharp-talking Calamity made gender-bending history in the old West.

Gender beliefs are not evil and they will always be with us. So let's hear it for women's dynamic relationships with the creative feminine. Remember Sylvia and Calamity Jane. Stay attuned to the snare of narrow stereotypic expectations. Step into your inherently female power and send gender messages that increase options and opportunities for everyone.

Image

If your vagina got dressed, what would it wear? Red high-tops and a Mets cap worn backwards.
Eve Ensler, writer, director, producer

To Crystal, hair was the most important thing on earth. She would never get married because you couldn't wear curlers in bed.
Edna O'Brien, Irish writer

Image is a part of belonging and a part of being unique. It expresses individuality and delineates group membership. Women are inundated with images and are bombarded with pressure to fit this month's flavor of perfection. Giving beauty advice is a mega-billion-dollar business. Here are two tips from one outrageously brilliant fashionista: "Never eat more than you can lift." And, "Never purchase beauty products in a hardware store." This is straight from Miss Piggy, the world's classiest porcine *femme fatale*.

Beauty and culture are in cahoots. Size, weight, hair, clothes, and skin become compelling and fascinating. The idealization of women's bodies at any point in time tends to be culturally conformist, one-form-only. The model changes often, but the acme of style, for as little as a season, is standardized and homogenized without much freedom to individualize and customize. The standards of judging beauty are not in the eyes of the beholder—they are embedded in our culture. As English writer Lady Mary Wortley Montagu opined, "If it was fashion to go naked, the face would be hardly observed."

Today's Western women talk about the pros and cons of hair color, hair extensions, tummy tucks, liposuction, breast implants, cosmetic surgery, and myriad treatments and injections. Instead of having lunch at noon, how about a quickie microdermabrasion treatment, chemical peel, and BOTOX® injection? As a social trend, becoming beautiful and remaining young has tsunami proportions with no body part left untouched. Where will it stop? What are the risks? What are the benefits? I say fall in love with your own body and get used to the idea that aging is inevitable. But, let's do lunch.

Creativity spurs acceptance of individual beauty and diversity and builds links to all women in order to celebrate feminine diversity.

Every woman has her own attractiveness. Unique body image is a woman's right. Singer, actor, and theme-park goddess Dolly Parton has built a career around her one-of-a-kind style. Here is Dolly's take on one of her best known physical attributes: "I was the first woman to burn my bra. It took the fire department four days to put it out." Women are at the heart of a world where they find their own ways to be energized and express their distinctive style.

For centuries, women either wore no underwear or wore undergarments constructed of steel rods and whale bones. In 1907, the word brassiere, derived from a French word for "upper arm" was playfully used in Vogue magazine. In 1913, the creative feminine muse spoke to Mary Phelps Jacobs. As a result, Mary was awarded a patent for the modern brassiere. Using silk handkerchiefs and pink ribbon, Mary constructed a bra and gave the world a whole new meaning for the word "support."

Before breasts were measured in inches, they were labeled small, medium, and large. Before A, B, and C cups, breasts were described as junior, maidenly, and mature. American vocalist Christina Aguilera advises adding this item to your have-to-have list. "I think everybody should have a great Wonderbra. There's so many ways to enhance them, everybody does it." Victorian bosoms, flapper flat chests, '50s sweater-girl cones, feminists sans bra, and Miraclebra cleavage are all part of the profile of the ins-and-outs of mammary silhouettes.

Historically, high fashion women's clothing was restrictive, uncomfortable, and impractical. This was important in distinguishing masculine from feminine, delineating both gender roles and social status. Current fashion can change overnight. Everyday changes in lifestyle, travel, technology, fitness, and fashion are immediately known and accessible. The glamour of film and television is no longer remote, but is easily and quickly available. Here is the essential clothes Q&A straight from fashion diva Joan Rivers. "Does fashion matter? Always, though not quite as much after death."

The emancipation of women and world wars encouraged women to adopt practical clothing and try out new styles. Women's participation in sports helped loosen the rigidity about clothes; they became more practical and less restrictive. Gilda Radner had the right idea. "I base most of my fashion sense on what doesn't itch." She was onto something. I have vowed never to wear shoes that hurt my feet.

Civilization requires clothes, and climate tends to support the notion. Clothes provide protection, ensure modesty, and exude sensuality. More than a fig leaf, clothes are powerful, nonverbal communicators. What we wear, and how and when we wear it, provides others with a shorthand message about the situation, the occasion, and the wearer of the outfit. Author Anne Hollander writes astutely about the power of clothes: "Clothes can suggest, persuade, connote, insinuate, or indeed lie and apply subtle pressure, while their wearer is speaking frankly and straightforwardly of other matters." Bend, twist, and suck it in; clothes are required.

Fashion may have been the first form of free speech and self-expression. I feel sure Imelda Marcos, beauty queen and political figure, would concur. Her fashion trademark was shoes, oodles of shoes. When her shoe inventory was overblown in the news, she quickly corrected the exaggeration. "I did not have three thousand pairs of shoes; I had one thousand and sixty." Tattoos, hoopskirts, blue jeans, little black dresses, high heels, and beehive hairdos are just some of the ways women express their creativity though fashion. Identity is announced in fashion style, and we all follow our creative muse when it comes to getting our particular look, but none of us ever want to be a "*Glamour* don't." Trust me.

Media

Television has proved that people will look at anything rather than each other.
Ann Landers, advice diva

You should always believe all you read in the newspapers, as this makes them more interesting.
Rose MacCaulay, English writer

Ah, the pervasiveness of media. Sounds like something that should be investigated with the results broadly disseminated. The media are persuasive partners in intricate relationships with creativity and everyday life. Image, influence, and intimacy instantaneously flow through the intervention of television, radio, newsprint, magazines, and the Internet. Mass messages and perspectives emerge through reality shows, sports competitions, sound bites, investigative reports, and screen crawls.

Media surrounds us with images of women: beautiful, thin, tall, and young. Billboards abound with close-up shots of super-sized female faces, torsos, and breasts that help to sell bread, beer, and barbecue grills. Apparently, female body parts can sell anything. Real-life women are beautiful, but the hyper-ideal slips into our consciousness and becomes an unreal measure of reality. The good news here is that when creatively enlightened men and women have behind-the-scenes power and artistic control, representations of women get a different spin and are portrayed as powerful, real, complex, and multi-faceted.

Nancy Drew was a media sensation from day one. Purported to be the creation of one woman, Nancy is in fact the composite brainchild of many authors. Nancy's ever young but always relevant persona sings with my kind of feminine creative spirit. Currently in her fifth text reincarnation, and fifth cinema and video presentation, Nancy is going strong. She is one of my favorite depictions of a young woman's self-reliance, courage, intelligence, and friendship. Nancy stays true to her muse, and I continue to find inspiration.

❧ Nancy Drew ❧

Never born, she will always live.

Nancy's passions are helping others and solving mysteries. In fashionable frocks and high heels, Nancy gets tied up, chases the bad guys, and explores dark and creepy places.

Nancy Drew enjoys the quest and thrives on adventure. With courage and competence, she tracks down thieves, finds lost treasure, and reunites separated families.

Family and friends are important. Nancy seeks advice from her attorney father and enjoys helping him on a case whenever possible. Bess and George, Nancy's two best girlfriends, are often a part of the adventure. Together the threesome works to untangle mysterious happenings. Puzzles, hidden maps, and coded messages engage their attention. Nancy is never baffled for long and is energized by the intriguing, often dangerous challenges that come her way. Nancy's independence and resourcefulness lead her to the clues that will crack the case.

—Mystery series created by Edward Stratemeyer in 1930, written by Carolyn Keene, pseudonym for numerous authors

Oprah Winfrey is a real-life superstar. Just like Nancy, working to improve the world for others is a part of her life ethos. Drew connects the clues, and Winfrey connects the many facets of media power. Winfrey's women-rallying message to live a better life through education and commitment is sent through every conceivable form of communication. Books, magazines, television, movies, radio, and the Internet—Oprah leaves no medium untapped. As a media icon, she stimulates change and awakens hope. As a world-class philanthropist, she entices her audience to make the world a better and safer place.

Media images of women's roles and their arenas of influence have mushroomed to reflect changes in our culture. In the good old days, a woman's media rep was either very, very good, or very, very bad. Catherine Aird, British author, summed it up, "If you can't be a good example, then you'll just have to be a horrible warning." Roles were confined to wife and mother, and the setting was always in the home. Not any more. Women are able to cross previously sacrosanct dividing lines. Families, friends, and careers are more diversely defined and intermingled in day-to-day reality. These new images instruct, inspire, and tempt our creativity.

In 1914, while on camelback trekking across a desert, English archeologist Gertrude Bell wrote, "You will find me a savage, for I have seen strange things, and they colour the mind." I think the same could be said of contemporary women who are travelers in the exotic lands of media. Creative women who master today's media teach us how to cook, entertain, repair a car, paint a house, and do just about anything. They explore the problems visited on, and created by humanity, and offer solutions. We can see others overcome obstacles, defy odds, and hop on fast tracks to dreams.

Cultural messages and assumptions, once entrenched, become invisible. We do not question or challenge what we do not notice. Actor Mary Newton said, "You know, I think I could have the cure to AIDS or cancer in my head, but that brain cell is filled instead with old dialogue from *The Brady Bunch*." That characterizes the insidious influence of media. They create artificial stars that are born and die in a seven-show season. They can rivet attention on isolated issues, create fictional characters that seem real, and replace real life and real dreams with sitcoms, fictionalized documentaries, and surreal survival contests.

WOMEN ADD DAZZLE
Humor

That is the best—to laugh with someone because you both think the same things are funny.

Gloria Vanderbilt, designer, artist, writer

I realize humor isn't for everyone. It's only for people who want to have fun, enjoy life, and feel alive.

Anne Wilson Schaef, author, lecturer

Laughter is one of the best things in life, and I like it sprinkled liberally throughout my day. When it comes to creative energy there is nothing like humor to jolt up the G-force. Bursts of giggles and guffaws affect emotions and thinking in ways that pure logic cannot. Laughter activates mental shifts and boundary expansions, triggering multiple parts of the brain. Humor enrolls thinking in the daft university of out-of-step possibilities.

Any woman who has had a mammogram can relate to author Jan King's witty comment. "Whoever thought up the word 'Mammogram'? Every time I hear it, I think I'm supposed to put my breast in an envelope and send it to someone." Women use humor as they use language: as a way to understand, be understood, and share experiences. Humor provides opportunities to keep conversation and connection going.

Women connect around issues of power and control as they comment on the cultural inequities they experience. Through humor, women expose restrictive stereotypes and challenge adverse and sexist norms. In *Outrageous Acts and Everyday Rebellions*, Gloria Steinem wrote about "seeing displayed on newsstands all over New York a *Screw* magazine centerfold of a woman with my face and glasses, a nude body drawn in labial detail, a collection of carefully drawn penises bordering the page and a headline instruction to, 'PIN THE COCK ON THE FEMINIST.' And my labia!" Bella Abzug's deadpan humor restored Steinem's spirits.

Women's humor builds cohesion-sharing attitudes, overlooking the unattractive and tolerating the unpleasant. Lighthearted humor harnesses absurdities and incongruities, whisks away barriers and burdens. I like singer Marie Osmond's advice, "If you are going to be able to look back on something and laugh about it, you might as well laugh about it now." Humor is a pleasurable experience that brings emotional lightness, resilience, and flexibility. Women explore similarities and differences as a way to bond with others and diffuse tension. We spin the magic of regained harmony and reconnection. Laughter reduces hostility and conflict. It is the perfect social super-glue, mending broken connections and cementing togetherness.

Laughter is better than snake oil. It is a healing force and a creative survival technique. Dolly Parton used humor to respond to an insulting remark: "I'm not offended by dumb blonde jokes because I know that I'm not dumb. I also know I'm not blonde."

A whoop-it-up chuckle enhances respiration, zipping more oxygen to the brain. So what? Well, tension in the muscular/skeletal system is decreased and as muscles relax, emotions lighten creating a feeling of ease. Humor lessens tenseness and alters perspectives. Laughter deflates fears and anxiety. It is almost impossible to laugh and worry at the same time. Author, Jessamyn West, reckoned, "A good time for laughing is when you can." Comic relief boosts the creative spirit and releases the stranglehold of tragedy and mistakes.

Ingenuity

For women there are, undoubtedly, great difficulties in the path,
but so much more to overcome. First, no woman should say, 'I am
but a woman!' But, 'A woman! What more could you ask to be?'
Maria Mitchell, astronomer

I have a brain and a uterus, and I use both.
Patricia Schroeder, former member of U.S. Congress

Through the ever-shifting panorama of culture, women's ingenuity prevails. Creativity's soul sister, ingenuity, is imbued with mischief, energy, and a desire to make things better, simpler, and easier. Creative vision entices action, and ingenuity strikes pay dirt.

Drench yourself. Plunge into whiz-bang ingenuity. Meet Mary Anderson. In 1905, Anderson's ingenuity swished, and streetcar windshield wipers whooshed into reality. Snow, rain, and sleet inspired her to make the streetcar driver's job easier and passengers' rides safer. The rubber-bladed swinging arm operated by the driver from the inside cleared the windshield. Ten years later, windshield wipers became standard equipment on cars.

Enthusiasm gleefully provokes ingenuity. "Too much of a good thing is wonderful!" Hollywood icon Mae West could have been talking about enthusiasm. Necessity-tweaked ingenuity hops, skips, and leaps through experiments, risks, and mistakes. Ideas, people, and resources rub elbows, stimulating ideas and awakening interests. Exuberant fun gets enterprise going and inveigles ingenuity into action. When I was interviewing Chere, I innocently asked how she went about setting goals. "Goals, that's navel gazing! Ideas jump into my head. I say them out loud, go after them, and process while I'm doing it." Let's hobnob with Chere for a moment.

My Creativity Smites Me Out of the Blue

An interview with a wild woman

Chere is a riveting catalyst. Hook up with Chere and you've met a jingling tambourine, filling the ether with spontaneous concertos of high-spirited imagination. Chere improvises ideas in staccato, rattling rhythm. Talking with Chere revs up your thinking. Did I mention that she is warm, enthusiastic, energetic, and stimulating?

She leads a fascinating life and is eager to talk about creativity. "I always let my muse guide me, everywhere, anywhere. I don't have time to be contemplative." When Chere had little money, she rented a farmhouse with no electricity or running water, and very little furniture. She scavenged to make it livable and beautiful, using feathers, branches and stones found in nature. Chere has the gift of making something magical out of the ordinary. She accomplishes anything that captures her fancy. Chere says she has had more than one hundred jobs. That does not surprise me. My favorite is snake wrestler—and if I know Chere—probably charmer, as well. I asked, "How do people respond to your creativity?"

"People respond positively when I'm not too manic or over the top."

Imagination is ingenuity's wily agent and accommodating cohort. Together they produce flights of fancy that give rise to soaring creative exploits. Imagination builds mercurial and fertile visions, and ingenuity gives them substance. Ingenuity and imagination prosper and flourish in the energy-soaked ether of enthusiasm.

"Many people are inventive, sometimes cleverly so. But real creativity begins with the drive to work on, and on, and on." Author Margueritte Harmon Bro could have been writing about inventor and entrepreneur Bette Nesmith Graham. Combine one blender, a bunch of mistakes, some tempera paint, and a desire to be efficient as an executive secretary. Season with ingenuity. In 1951, Graham invented a product to paint over typos. When word got out, typists everywhere wanted a bottle of Mistake Out, later renamed White Out. In 1976, the Liquid Paper business turned out twenty-five million bottles. Bette sold the corporation in 1980, for $47.5 million.

Some women spin wool into yarn. Twentieth century alchemist Stephanie Louise Kwolek ingeniously spun a cloudy, fluid polymer into an incredible, strong synthetic fiber. Known as Kevlar®, it is ounce-for-ounce five times stronger than steel. As a child, Stephanie loved fabrics and sewing and dreamed of being a fashion designer. With clever resourcefulness she transformed her vision into a wish come true; Kevlar is used to make bulletproof vests and flame-resistant helmets. Kwolek obtained 28 patents as a research scientist and has been inducted into the National Inventors Hall of Fame.

"Whatever women do they must do twice as well as men to be thought half as good. Luckily, this is not difficult." Charlotte Whitton, feminist and politician, could have been referring to inventive women. A few not-so-surprising things invented by women are zigzag sewing machines, rolling pins, permanent waves for hair, and canister vacuums. Some oh-so-surprising things patented by women are the car heater, circular saw, elevated railway, engine muffler, submarine telescope, and flat-bottomed paper bag making machine.

Humor and ingenuity inflate the inner tube of creative consciousness and float it in streams of history and culture. Creativity quickens in the slipstream of the creative feminine. At the beginning of history and culture, there was Eve. This powerful archetype inaugurated some snazzy expressions of wild-woman creativity.

✑ Eve ✑

Never born, she will always live.

Garden of Eden Press: Fearless female talks to serpent, finds tree, eats fruit, and then shares with partner. The headline is true. Eve confirms it. She did talk to the cold-blooded, legless reptile, and she warns, "Beware of the snake in the grass." As for apples, she suggests making a pie.

Fashion World Magazine: Eve, the original couturiere, is incredibly inventive. When she noticed her nudity, she improvised some drapery and conjured up the concept of clothes. As the premier fashion designer, Eve's inaugural runway theme was the fig leaf.

Eve! The Original Woman: Eve, prototypic wild woman, is no saint. She personifies humanity's powerful urge to create and sustain life. Eve's essence as a role model is ingenuity driven by the pursuit of knowledge, experimentation, and risk-taking.

First celebrity, first couturier, first chef—Eve's initiative in all of us continues to create meaningful response to change. That little bit of her in each of us urges us to venture into realms of wondrous possibility. Author Annie Dillard says it just right, "The dedicated life is worth living. You must give with your whole heart." Creatively daring women expand worlds, extend boundaries, and cross barriers.

Chapter Four

Women Connect

One of the oldest human needs is having someone to wonder where you are when you don't come home at night.

—Margaret Mead, cultural anthropologist, writer

It seems to me that trying to live without friends is like milking a bear to get cream for your morning coffee. It is a whole lot of trouble, and then not worth much after you get it.

—Zora Neale Hurston, American author

*A*s we get ready to jump into creativity, remember it is everywhere and in each of us. Thank goodness, there is no need to stock up on or conserve creativity, the original renewable resource. Social activist Ethel Percy Andrus gave voice to creativity's sustainable nature. "What I spent is gone; what I kept, I lost; but what I gave away will be mine forever."

The feminine creative has a message. Embrace relationships. As a woman in relationships with women, I have benefited from being a daughter, sister, niece, aunt, friend, and colleague. In relationships, I am able to nurture and be nurtured, love and be loved, teach and learn. Building relationships connects us. So hook up, plug into, join league with, hitch on, and go partners. Make the leap.

Penny's nurturing creativity springs from a profound connection with her Greek heritage. Her abiding sense of the ancient place that gave birth to her ancestors influences her spirituality and resonant sense of family connection. She says, "Knowing your roots nourishes your soul and strengthens your passion, compassion, and creativity." For Penny, family is an oasis where faith and mutual respect are ever available to replenish thirsty souls.

⪗ A Little House on the Beach ⪘

An interview with a wild woman

"Love big, and do what warms you," Penny says. "What we create begins with who we are in our heart of hearts." Her creative feminine communicates belief in goodness, beauty, and people. Family is at the center of Penny's spirituality, passion, and dreams. What does she yearn for? She wants her two sons on the right path, a close connection with her husband, their livelihood in place, and a little house on the beach where it all comes together. I asked Penny to share her wisdom. "Take time to find your voice," Penny says. Hers sings with confidence, sincerity, and spirituality.

Capitalizing on her distinctive blend of beliefs and talents, Penny has created a family built on affectionate care. Her heart-warmed connections provide moorings for creative, collaborative energy.

If you, like me, have some great connections with women, take a minute. Let your mind and heart wander. Appreciate a standout relationship. My best high school friend, Kay, and I were inseparable. We shared a mild interest in academics, a serious pursuit of fun, and we were slightly rebellious. Together, we had a ball, got into trouble, and did some screwy stuff. Together is the important word. Together we played hooky, got caught, and went to detention. Forever in tune, we decided to color our hair using green food coloring and had ghastly emerald shimmers for weeks. One semester, we decided not to participate in physical education, figuring that one F was not that bad. Kay and I had lots of fun together.

FAMILIAL BOUNTY

Family is an accident … They don't mean to get on your nerves.
They don't even mean to be your family, they just are.
Marsha Norman, Pulitzer Prize-winning author

Like all the best families, we have our share of eccentricities,
of impetuous and wayward youngsters and of family
disagreements.
Elizabeth Windsor, Queen of the United Kingdom of Great
Britain and Northern Ireland

Families give life. Healthy families encourage and affirm relational connections. Through example, they show us how to maintain a positive outlook. They nurture, protect, and guide children and vulnerable family members. That is an enormous job requiring lots of creativity. So whatever the mix of talent, ambition, custom, and caprice a family concocts, creativity is essential. Families going about the business of being a family are surely dynamos of creative potency and stamina.

There is universality to the ways women go about being in families. Women are more likely than men to be involved with family members, and they carry out the majority of contact and exchanges between generations. Daughters, sisters, mothers, grandmothers, aunts, nieces, wives, mothers-in-law, and daughters-in-law maintain family connections and traditions. Pioneer aviator Amelia Earhart made the point beautifully. "Better do a good deed near at home than go far away to burn incense." My friend Cindy has a flair for enlivening family connections and a knack for ramping up tradition. Enjoy a moment with Cindy.

✑ **Everybody on the Bus** ✑

An interview with a wild woman

Cindy is the champion organizer of family events and spontaneous instigator of casual dinners with friends. She loves bringing people together, making things happen, and having fun. An exuberant communicator and connector, Cindy mobilizes creativity to max the pleasure and ditch the fuss. Everyone gets to have a good time.

Twenty-seven in-laws from out of town were coming for Christmas. Cindy was undaunted. With get-out-of-town ingenuity, she hired a tour bus and the rest just fell into place. The result was relaxed holiday cheer. Her family sang carols, viewed Christmas lights, and joyously concluded with margaritas and fajitas at a local Mexican hotspot. *¡Feliz Navidad!*

Grandmothers

A home without a grandmother is like an egg without salt.
Florence King, Mississippi author

Alive with intergenerational energy, grandmothers strengthen families and stabilize the future for children and grandchildren. With comforting talents and deep-seated wisdom, they help rear the young as they pass on traditions and skills. Grandma Lee, my Dad's mother, embroidered and crocheted like a wild-woman. She embellished pillowcases, sheets, tablecloths, and napkins. Anything you could take needle and thread to was fair game for Lee. She crocheted baby clothes, tablecloths, and doilies. None of that captured my five-year-old fancy, but then she crocheted the lacy white dress for me. I still love that dress and vividly remember how beautiful I felt when I had it on and how the hem tickled my knees.

From instrumental to sentimental, grandmothers are heart-warming sources of support. Grandmothers enrich the lives of grandchildren. As life expectancy lengthens, the role of grandmother expands. More women will become grandmothers and many will see their grandchildren's children. Having two, or even three, generations of grandmothers in a family is not uncommon. Most women with children will spend half of their lives as grandmothers.

Grandmothers have the power to send the message that life is good. Writer Ernestine Ulmer imparted some pure granny wisdom. "Life is uncertain. Eat dessert first." Grandmothers' accomplishments and values inspire grandchildren with possibilities. They have knowledge, experience, advice, and skill. As repositories of family history and rituals, Granny, Nana, Bubbe, Abuela, Grandma, and Memere forge links that join generations in a common view of the future.

Mothers

Suddenly there she was. And I was no longer pregnant; I was a mother. I never believed in miracles before.

Ellen Greene, actor

Mothers give birth to and nurture the next generation. They are powerful and influential players in the ancestral drama of family heritage. Immersed in the everyday world of family, their familial relationships are crucial for generational continuity and the transmission of culture. Motherhood is a series of transitions with an ongoing ever-upward learning curve. There is no retirement, no vacation, no holiday, and no time off for good behavior. Moms mother forever.

Mothers are the lynchpins of civilization's future. They are caretakers, role models, and instructors. My mom is a storyteller. As a child she held friends rapt with her stories. Her trick was to weave everyone into the story. When I was little, Mom did the same thing with my friends. They would call out to her, "make me strong" or "let me be a princess." At bedtime, Mom would tell me the continuing saga of the little red-haired girl. I could ask for a long story, sad story, or a scary story, knowing that it would always be about me and always end happily ever after. Mom's magic always began with, "Once upon a time there was a . . ." Mothers guide and nurture their children to become adults that can respond to adversity with resilience. My mom's stories did that for me. Louise Erdrich, best-selling author, captured her memories of these experiences. Erdrich wrote, "I want to lean into her like the wheat leans into the wind."

Traditionally, mothers have raised daughters to be wives and mothers. The spirals of women's development are reflected in mother-daughter relationships. Independence, education, career, marriage, and children are some of the areas that mothers and daughters may experience as differences or conflicts. Bonnie Hunt, actor, producer, director, and writer, told this story. "My mom gave me a card on my wedding day and, you know, I'm on my honeymoon, it's the first night and I open up the card that my mother handed me at the end of the night and there's a little quarter taped in it and at the bottom it say, 'If you don't like him, call me. I'll come get you.'" Untangling the wispy threads of their own needs, challenges, and unfulfilled dreams can challenge mothers' perspectives and expectations.

Suffragist Ann Reeves Jarvis wanted women to be recognized for their work as mothers. After she died on May 10, 1908, her daughter, Anna Marie Jarvis, took on her mother's desire to establish a nationally recognized day in honor of all mothers. Anna dedicated her life and employed her talents to attain her mother's lifelong dream. She wrote letters, lectured, and campaigned. Successful in 1914, the second Sunday in May is reserved for the celebration of Mother's Day.

Culture holds mothers to the highest standards of perfection and selflessness. Mothers are expected to provide children with physical safety, nurturing, and an environment that enhances the mind and the ability to think. Motherhood is demanding yet fulfilling, exhilarating yet exhausting, frightening yet joyful.

Daughters

When I stopped seeing my mother with the eyes of a child, I saw the woman who helped me give birth to myself.
Nancy Friday, author, social commentator

All women are born daughters. Being a daughter is the first relationship in a woman's life. In this complex and significant role, women gather clues about what it means to be a woman. The primal nature of daughter-mother relationships builds in the desire to be different, the fear that nothing will change, and the anxiety of future separation. I loved the scene in *Terms of Endearment* when Emma and her mother, Aurora, are hugging goodbye before Emma leaves town with her husband. Emma pulls out of the hug and says, "Mama, that's the first time I stopped hugging first. I like that."

When daughters move to a relationship of greater equality and announce their independence as an adult, their relationships with their mothers shift. In our ever-changing daughter-mother relationships, we refine, edit, rewrite, elaborate, and pare down our views of ourselves and our mothers. Remaining connected, but separate and independent, a mother can be a source of friction and source of strength. Conflict, perseverance, rebellion, education, and experience instigate the communication and adaptation needed to reshape relationships and sustain connections.

Sisters

What surprised me was that within a family, the voices of sisters as they're talking are virtually always the same.
Elizabeth Fisher, author

A baby sister is nicer than a goat. You'll get used to her.
Lynne Alpern and Esther Blumenfeld, authors

The best sound in the world is sisters laughing together. Sisters have special opportunities to collect stories of the past, handle happy times, work through problems, and share the grief of family loss. That is just the way it is for my sister Gina and me. Our connection is a close and wondrous bond filled with celebration and joy. We have three-hour lunches and then talk for hours again that same evening. She and I emptied our family house, filled with fifty years of stuff, in a week, and we redecorated Mom's bedroom in a day. We always know the right thing to give each other for birthdays and Christmas, sometimes we get the same thing. English writer Charlotte Brontë expressed it well. "You know full as well as I do the value of sisters' affections for each other; there is nothing like it in this world."

Historically and culturally, sisters tend to have the closest relation-ships. Evolving over time, the sister connection is an intense attach-ment characterized by a unique set of shared family experiences with ties to childhood. Given women's longevity, the relationship in life that is most likely to last the longest is between sisters. They also can become each others' most happy companions in old age.

Author Patricia Volk writes, "I know some sisters who only see each other on Mother's Day and some who will never speak again. But most are like my sister and me . . . linked by volatile love, best friends who make other best friends ever so slightly less best." Although competition, rivalry, and parental favoritism can make for estrangement, sibships last a lifetime. Genetically and contex-tually, sisters share their lives. They can become both mirror and role model. In this complex, influential, and intimate relationship, sisters almost always see reflections of some part of themselves.

Other Mothers

"What I'm looking for is a blessing that's not in disguise."
Kitty O'Neill Collins, author

Here is one more category that I think broadens our understand-ing of women's ability to connect in special ways. I call them "other-mothers." They become our mothers by way of our friendship with their daughters. These allies and co-conspirators show the way to make circumstances responsive to our needs. Their attention and generosity tells us that we are wonderfully important.

Marian Wright Edelman, lawyer and children's advocate, described the essence of other-mothering with these words. "We must not, in trying to think about how we can make a big difference, ignore the small daily difference we can make which, over time, add up to big differences we often cannot foresee." Other-mothers create special bonds with us. As benefactors, these women love us and validate our aspirations. They are wise women who encourage us and support our dreams.

Mary, the mother of my first-ever best friend, Kathleen, would always tell my mother that I should have been her daughter. Mary would say, "Hilda is just like me. Let her come over anytime." I thought Mary was super. Her comments made me feel special. Charlotte, the mother of Alice, my next-door-neighbor best friend, taught me how to knit. This was a huge undertaking as Charlotte is right-handed, and I am a lefty. I would work away at my practice piece, snarl the yarn, drop stitches, and do other unspeakable things to my growing tangle of wool. Charlotte would undo, redo, and show me again. I ended up loving the orderliness of the process and made quite a few beautifully executed sweaters.

RELATIONAL JUJU

We don't accomplish anything in this world alone ... and whatever happens is the result of the whole tapestry of one's life and all the weavings of individual threads from one to another that creates something.

Sandra Day O'Connor, retired Supreme Court Justice

Each contact with a human being is so rare, so precious, one should preserve it.

Anais Nin, French-born American writer

Laura Petrie has relational juju. I would know because in the 1960s I made a study of Laura. Every week for thirty minutes I would watch to see how she and her husband, Rob, let us know how perfectly wild they were for each other. I liked the give-and-take camaraderie she shared with her best friend as they took turns being the wise one or the wacky one. I studied her joyous, game-for-anything participation in the life of her suburban community.

✀ Laura Petrie ✀

Never born, she will always live.

Yes, she is beautiful and talented, but Laura Petrie is also sensible and clever. Always on the lookout for ways to use her intelligence and know-how, Laura's irresistible charm makes life interesting. Laura's living and dining rooms are often filled with friends for dinner, family get-togethers, play rehearsals, and talent show tryouts. There always seems to be lots of happy people, singing, dancing, laughing, and enjoying life. A force of life and happiness, Laura's conviviality is contagious.

—*The Dick Van Dyke Show* created by Carl Reiner in 1961

I loved Laura Petrie then, and I still do. Laura's skill in connecting with friends and community nourishes creative process—hers and theirs. Conversation, exchange of ideas, and shared experiences groove on the give-and-take alliances that hatch comfort, expressiveness, empathy, fun, and mutuality. Connection multiplies potential and animates creativity.

Women approach connection informed by intuitive understandings of context. They seek environments that encourage friendships and safeguard kinships. Their diverse collaborations spark opportunities. Women instinctively respect individual needs, differences, and boundaries and have the empathy to seek out new chums and build lasting alliances.

"Yikes! We've known each other so long." Steadfast girlfriends get to say that to each other a lot. Socially skilled women construct durable networks of lasting relationships that are built on close associations. Intimacy conveys an appreciation of reciprocal sharing and brings depth and warmth to relationships.

Women and creativity are strong allies, working in harmony to enhance relational connections. Most creatively interconnected women would totally get what social activist Ethel Percy Andrus wrote. "The human contribution is the essential ingredient." Lasting or casual, relationships are life's blood, with the potential to positively impact physical health and emotional well being. These ties begin and are shaped by our initial bond with parents. Friendships, dating, committed partnerships, marriage, and all other human affiliations follow with the potential to support creative growth.

Friendship

Yes'm old friends is always best, 'less you can catch a new one
that's fits to make an old one out of.
Sarah Orme Jewett, American novelist

I do not want people to be very agreeable, as it saves me the
trouble of liking them a great deal.
Jane Austen, English novelist

Friends are life's goodwill ambassadors. A map of our friendships illustrates the landscape of our interests, joy, pain, and sharing. Interactions with friends—the beginnings, endings, and all that is in between—depict our involvement with life. As growth and change occur, friendship additions and losses reflect the numerous byways of life's unfolding journey.

I spent twenty years working with my friend Coleta. When my career morphed and took off in a new direction, our working lives no longer overlapped. So we didn't see each other for about seven years. Then, Coleta sent me a birthday card, I called her, and we had lunch. The friendship had not lost its strength. We laughed, talked, remembered, and shared new interests. Hours later we were still yakking it up.

Girls, girls, girls. Our friendly oxytocin and superb verbal skills give us an edge in the friend-making game. Girls tend to be adept at relational skills and learn to communicate one-on-one early in life. They value the importance of listening, maintaining harmony, and avoiding conflict. Female best friends focus on relational factors and spend time together talking about mutual interests. Some engage in long, intimate conversations about personally significant events, others listen attentively. As staunch allies, the most highly valued girlfriends provide support and cheer our successes.

From day one, girls just seem to know how to create connections. Empathic women are attuned to the warmth of human closeness that arises from sensitivity to, and respect for, others. Female friends spend time talking and listening; they stress the importance of equal measures of emotion and intellect in their friendships. Confiding, understanding, and reassuring are part of being a supportive friend.

Gertrude Stein and Alice Toklas shared a life-partnership filled with creative rapport. Gertrude was "Lovey" to Alice, and Alice was "Pussy" to Gertrude. These great friends met in 1906 and, for thirty-nine years, lived together in Paris. Alice and Gertrude agreed on many things. That Gertrude was a genius was their foremost shared belief. Among the many mutually agreeable notions was an abundance of great food and a disinclination to do anything that did not amuse them, such as driving in reverse. They shared a great aversion to entertaining boring writers and artists. Since Alice got up early in the morning and Gertrude wrote late into the night, Gertrude would leave affectionate notes to perk up Alice's mornings. Alice believed that Gertrude was immortal, so she opted for Catholicism to ensure that in the afterlife she would be reunited with Gertrude.

Women tend to form intimate and lasting relationships. Intuitively empathic women know that to have friends, you must be a friend, and that relationships are not instantaneous. Congenial and accessible confidants share important feelings and thoughts, building deeply committed relationships. Feminist writer, Louise Berkinow, touched on the respectful closeness that women can create in their friendships. "Female friendships that work are relationships in which women help each other to belong to themselves." It takes time to develop the trust needed to achieve a sense of connection and relationship. Going through tough times together brings depth and breadth to relationships. The best of friends are allies who sympathize with us and provide emotional intimacy and companionship, rain or shine. They know us and remain fond of us!

Congenial confederates aid and abet the daring exploits of growing up and growing wise. Friends play an important role in our sense of well-being and have a positive impact on life. We rely on a friend as someone who cares and who will affirm and support us. Friendships shape and influence who we are and who we might become. They soothe our inner worlds, offer solace, and nourish emotional growth.

Jane and I were sitting together waiting for a committee meeting to start. We did not know each other well, so we chatted about day-to-day stuff. I asked about her plans for the summer. She told me about doll making and how important it was in her life. I have not seen Jane since our committee work together was completed, but I continue to feel the connection of our shared moment.

✑ Circle of Friends ✑

An interview with a wild woman

With skilled hands, doll makers transform bits and pieces of materials into manifestations of internal ideas. Doll making includes the shaping of head and hands and the sculpting and depiction of the face and personality of every doll. Clothes are designed and sewn to establish the persona of each unique creation. Making dolls is a study of real people with the results made known through the countenance of each doll.

Jane is a part of a small group of women who travel from afar to come together to learn this artisan craft. For a cluster of days, they are connected in an intense and intimate experience.

This trip was to have additional meaning for Jane. The doll she envisioned would look like her son who had died the year before. Jane said researching the project had provided a safe and creative way to explore memories. She wisely understood that there were many paths of memories too painful to touch. The structure of doll making, the magic of creative process, and the warmth of friends provided Jane with ways to live with the loss of a child.

Jane trusted her circle of friends. Author Lois Wyse put into words the magic of women coming together. "A good friend is a connection to life—a tie to the past, a road to the future, a key to sanity in a totally insane world." Women tend to rely on friends for emotional support. Women who are more socially active may live at least one or two years longer than women who are more socially isolated. Having someone you can turn to in a time of need is invaluable. A reliable ally can embolden courage and buoy resilience. Healthy friendships are a balm for isolation and loneliness. Sharing with a friend boosts emotional well-being.

Hanging out with friends is beneficial, contributing to emotional vitality and good health. With friends, we are able to sample the full range of feelings. Friendship becomes more important as we age, protecting us from isolation. Author Annie Gottlieb portrayed one of the best reasons to make friends. "We challenge one another to be funnier and smarter. . . . It's the way friends make love to one another." Friends help us maintain independence, promote self-esteem and encourage social activity. Companions and cohorts vitalize feelings of competence and satisfaction with life. They offer sustaining help, understanding, and affirmation.

Pals and sidekicks are an integral part of a life span. Friendships are important at every age. Needs change as women grow from little girls to matriarchs. Friendships develop and shift over time, often coinciding with life events such as marriage, divorce, remarriage, retirement, diminished health, widowhood, or relocation. Our comrades in friendship provide companionship and emotional understanding. Friends lift our game and engage our passion for life.

Marriage and Divorce

If love never means having to say you're sorry, then marriage means always having to say everything twice.
Estelle Getty, actor, maverick mother, television trailblazer

Love involves a peculiar unfathomable combination of under-standing and misunderstanding.
Diane Arbus, American photographer

Marriage doesn't necessarily make you happy, it only makes you married. Historically, for the upper classes, marriage was a political and economic institution, devised to secure property rights and protect bloodlines. It was not intended for individual benefit. Personality, attractiveness, and love were on the bottom of the priority list. Divorce was rarely an option.

Enlightenment, individualism, and prosperity brought change. The new marital ideal required that couples invest emotional energy in each other and their children, rather than their birth families. New emphasis was placed on companionship, intimacy, and privacy. Marriage changed from a financial and political con-venience to a romantically cherished ideal. Once armed with the power of choice, divorce became an option and a reality.

Beginning in the 1960s, the cultural vision of a Western mar-riage shifted yet again. Despite efforts to maintain traditional per-spectives, the concept of what marriage encompasses exploded, forming surprising new shapes and variations. It was no longer an indication of adulthood or the sole way to organize the lives of children. Love, sexuality, and sexual orientation were redefined.

The status of women within marriage has changed and continues to evolve. Women have more options while married and fewer obstacles to divorce. Educational and career advances have increased women's financial independence. For women, marriage no longer has to be an economically dependent relationship.

Divorce, American style, with an assist from Celebrityland, hatched a new concept—the serial bride. "I've married a few people I shouldn't have, but haven't we all?" With five husbands under her belt, Mamie Van Doren, B-movie sex-bomb, knew what she was talking about. In Hollywood, the divorce record holder for women is Zsa Zsa Gabor with nine walks down the aisle. Elizabeth Taylor has been married eight times but to only seven husbands.

Hollywood nonesuch Diane Keaton has a different take on marriage. With four well-known significant others to her credit, Academy-award winning Keaton says she has definitely shut the door on marriage. Acknowledging that marriage requires a lot of trade-offs and concession, she knows it is not for her. "I'm attracted to men, and I love playing around with them. But a life together? You have to be someone who can compromise." In *The Cabin in the Cotton*, I think Bette Davis, another Oscar winner, captured some of Keaton's take on marriage when, as Madge, she confidently drawled, "I'd love to kiss ya, but I just washed my hair."

People live longer, marry later, divorce sooner, and are just as likely to live together as they are to marry. Marriage is no longer the only significant milestone of adulthood or the initial rite of sexual relationships. Growing numbers of couples in our culture choose to live together rather than marry. High rates of divorce, increased longevity, and the lessening of the stigma for cohabitation play a part in less traditional choices.

Women buy most of the self-help books about marriage and relationships and initiate most marital therapy. "Divorce is only less painful than the need for a divorce." So wrote feminist Jane O'Reilly. Still, women file for divorce twice as often as men. Marriage remains the basic family unit but divorce is likely to sever important family bonds, as well as linkages between children and the paternal side of the family.

In spite of those changes, marriage still has some sticking power. Sometimes love is all you need. Artist Lynda Barry appreciated the power of love. "If it is your time, love will track you down like a cruise missile." Just as racially mixed couples fought for the legality of their relationships, today lesbian and gay couples seek recognition for their unions. The bonds of marriage, loving or legal, are changing.

COMMUNITY PIZZAZZ

Amid all the easily loved darlings of Charlie Brown's circle, obstreperous Lucy holds a special place in my heart. She fusses and fumes and she carps and complains. That's because Lucy cares. And it's the caring that counts.
Judith Crist, American film critic

Sharing is sometimes more demanding than giving.
Mary Catherine Bateson, writer, cultural anthropologist

Teamwork and the combined strength of a community can inspire creative solutions. Community is the concept of strength in numbers, part of humanity's drive to connect and create. Communities evoke a sense of closeness, belonging, sharing, and caring. Productive communities are the result of energy, commitment, skill, and talent. The respect, compassion, and emotional bonds that arise increase the sum of creative energy and output.

Communities have a dynamic influence on relational connections. They are vital in our endeavors to find meaning and creative fulfillment in the midst of the happenstance of life. In working, learning, and creating together, we have impact on others, and connections with others affect us. Interactions tied to positive shared commitment foster mutual growth, enriched knowledge, and deepened skill.

Talk-show host Virginia Graham's observation is applicable to team and community endeavors. "Good shot, bad luck, and hell are the five basic words to be used in a game of tennis, though these, can be amplified slightly." Cooperation and relational connection energize communities, as do passionately shared goals and interests. Communities are shaped by common concerns, problems, and pursuits. Whether socially or professionally focused, communities offer opportunities for people to work, learn, and play together.

Community involvement activates the urge for individuals to be creative. As communities observe, think, act, adapt, and reflect, they square-up and refine their creative pursuits. Provisional decisions are a part of the flow of a community's effort. When we interact in groups, information gets shared. Good ideas flourish, and so-so or bad ideas get shot down or ignored.

Creativity is a natural part of communities. Members build things and solve problems. In the process of developing and sustaining a community, we learn and invent. We must innovate as amity, affiliation, and accomplishment are established. Ability to clarify intentions and work toward common goals is essential. Artful attention to the messy process of gathering resources and assessing risks takes place in the context of initiative and needs.

Diversity and challenge can stimulate a community's creative thought and effective communication. Regina's architect brain sees order in chaos and innovation as a path to better futures. Regina has traveled many roads in her career. She says, "As I have changed, my creativity has changed. The more I challenge myself, the more self-assured I feel. I have the confidence to try. Once you start down the court, just shoot; when on the path, go with the divine flow."

✌ Fulfilling Potential ✌

An interview with a wild woman

One of Regina's career paths centered on an innovative program designed to help impoverished and unemployed persons become self-sufficient. This not-for-profit organization, in partnership with an international foundation, makes micro-loans to people without financial resources who have good ideas and a desire to work and be independent.

Predominantly women, the recipients are determined to become self-reliant. Along with a small loan, participants are provided with business tools and collegial support. Small support groups work together as each member's business is planned and marketed and their loans are repaid. Most become self-employed.

Regina's creative expertise builds stronger communities. Like Regina, members of a productive community are drawn together to collaborate and frame broader horizons. By doing, practicing, experimenting, and capitalizing on successful, empowering experiences we build upbeat community connection.

Individuals in forward thinking communities cooperate. Personal responsibility plus shared emotional and intellectual stakes generate a sense of cohesiveness. New Jersey Superior Court Justice Marianne Espinosa expressed the essence of community spirit when she said, "Often the best way to win is to forget to keep score." Community is a mixture of openness, trust, and a sense of mutuality, which is underscored by a willingness to listen, balanced obligation, and reliable action.

Enlightened women realize that the world is interactive. Search, discovery, and creativity bring competence, commitment, and fun to human experience. Mindful of the power of creativity, women develop and sustain flourishing communities.

In Sanskrit, the word *Ananya* means, "like whom there is no other." The Ananya Dance Theater is a treasure in our universe like no other. Mission drives this all female company of artists. Diverse in age, race, nationality, and sexual orientation, Ananya women create dance where every woman feels valued, cherished, and challenged. They believe that, through movement, individual dreams and desires are articulated. This sisterhood of artists works from the conviction that the search for artistic excellence builds strong communities and generates strength and beauty.

Like the artists of Ananya, women will instigate the spirit of community where none exists. Why is that a good idea? Feminist author Brenda Ueland has the answer. "Why should we use all of our creative powers ...? Because there is nothing that makes people so generous, joyful, lively, bold, and compassionate, so indifferent to fighting and the accumulation of objects and money." Women's holistic, relational, and contextual thinking lends itself to communal approaches to much of life.

Chapter Five

Women
Learn

Nothing, of course, begins at the time you think it did.

—Lillian Hellman, American playwright

We are not what we know but what we are willing to learn.

—Mary Catherine Bateson, writer, cultural anthropologist

Oh, to have traveled with Maria Mitchell. Professor Mitchell's idea of a great field trip was a 2,000-mile train journey from New York to Colorado to see a total solar eclipse. July heat, lost luggage, and accommodations in a tent were part of the learning adventure. With telescopes pointed towards the heavens for exactly two minutes and forty seconds, the sky had no limits for the young women of Vassar and their teacher, Miss Mitchell.

Maria Mitchell kindled fires that glowed with a love of learning. She set a high standard of intellectual achievement, even though the students were "only women." Mitchell believed out in the field, hands-on experiences couldn't be beat. She loved to ask her Vassar students, "Did you learn that from a book, or did you observe it yourself?"

Astronomer Maria Mitchell (1818–1889) was a lifelong learner. She created a life filled with opportunities to discover, learn, and use knowledge. At age twenty-nine, while studying the night sky, she caught sight of the comet that would be named Miss Mitchell's Comet. After teaching at Vassar for some time, she determined that her salary was significantly less than younger and less experienced male professors. She demanded, and received, a pay raise. As an abolitionist, she refused to wear cotton in protest of slavery, and as a believer in women's rights she co-founded the American Association for the Advancement of Women.

Intuitive brains and oxytocin-laced longevity influence learning and creativity. Of course women are rational and objective, but we love to stir in the personal. This affects how we take in and process information and how we respond. I know that, for me, the feeling piece is critical. I must feel rapport with the instructor, exhilarated by context, fascinated with a concept, or the need to attain information or a skill. Thinking and deciding almost always follow the lead of my feelings. Just like Mitchell, we each develop our own blend of thinking, feeling, and deciding.

Learning is not a one-way stream from teacher to student. Women have long intuited that students learn from each other and that instructors most certainly learn from their pupils. Maria Montessori, early childhood education innovator, said it well. "I studied my children, and they taught me how to teach them." Women create learning environments with give-and-take in mind. We attend to the influence of connection and community on learning.

In describing the interconnectedness of life and learning, Professor K. Patricia Cross wrote, "Learning is not so much an additive process, with new learning simply piling up on top of existing knowledge, as it is an active process in which the connections are constantly changing and the structure reformatted." While keeping the whole and the parts in mind, the creative feminine orchestrates spillover and overlap. Creativity and learning go hand-in-hand as new information and innovation lure us into developing our brains. In *All About Eve*, Bette Davis got the party rolling with this famous Margo Channing phrase: "Fasten your seatbelts, it's going to be a bumpy night." My imagination sees this as a preamble to a night on the town with creativity and learning. Grab your red paint, and let's go.

INVESTMENT
Brains

If you have formed the habit of checking on every new diet that comes along, you will find that, mercifully, they all blur together, leaving you with only one definite piece of information: french-fried potatoes are out.

Jean Kerr, writer, lyricist

Shaped a little like a loaf of French country bread, our brain is a crowded chemistry lab, bustling with nonstop neural conversations.

Diane Ackerman, naturalist, poet, author

Brains thrive on generous deposits of information and experience. Learning is money in the bank and a lifetime process. So invest regularly and maintain an active and diverse portfolio.

Healthy brains enjoy learning and are capable of learning throughout life. Our inventive brains thrive on provocation and encouragement. Learning is the brain on a skateboard, and gray matter is the playground for neural acrobatics. Ideas whiz through our wrinkled, convoluted brains. Skateboarding brains dare to suspend what they think they know in pursuit of what might be learned.

Learning thrives on a diet rich in challenging problems, mental mazes, and complex codes to decipher. In *Auntie Mame*, Rosalind Russell proclaims, "Live! Life's a banquet and most poor suckers are starving to death." Ina Garten, of *The Barefoot Contessa*, whisks up culinary magic. I know how to make great scrambled eggs, but by watching Ina I learn to ramp up a basic skill. Got eggs? Why not whip up a wild-mushroom and three cheese frittata? I love it when she asks, "Who wouldn't like that?" Or, "How easy is that?" Two of my favorite femmes teach us the joys of digging into life's bounty.

Creative brains are rowdy instigators in search of novelty and diversity. Just recently I painted silvery moons and stars on the ceiling of my sunroom. When friends asked what made me think to do that, I tell them about Aunt Edith, Mom's red-haired, wild-woman older sister. I was seven when I discovered my favorite aunt painting pink polka-dots across the floor and ceiling of her porch. She taught through example how to follow whimsy. Our over-the-top brains love to learn and elaborate. Guided by intelligence and experience, our creative feminine keeps our brain happily humming.

Women handle problems and reality just fine. Our intuitive brains integrate facts and skills and then conceive, plan, predict, risk, respond, and follow through. Women are parallel operators, stimulated by variety and energized by surprise. Well-connected female brains snap to quick solutions with well-informed intuition and bring order even while multi-tasking. I like the way American novelist Edna Ferber conveyed the vibe of smart-thinking women. "I may not know much. Her tone utterly belied the words; her tone told you that not only did she know much, but all." When we know, we really know.

"Only people who die very young learn all they really need to know in kindergarten." Wendy Kaminer, lawyer, journalist, and social critic got it right. I'll bet life-long learner Maggie Kuhn would agree. While teaching at the YWCA, Kuhn educated women about birth control and sexual pleasure. Her battle cry was "Leave safety behind. Put you body on the line. Stand before the people you fear, and speak your mind." Believing that old age was filled with strength, survivorship, and triumph, she founded The Gray Panthers. Maggie was a fighter for education, human rights, social and economic justice, and global peace. When asked why she never married, Kuhn wisecracked, "Sheer luck."

Maggie is on the top of my list of people to have at a fantasy dinner. She glowed with a spirited feminine creative and was a passionate investor in her own and others' learning. The dividend was social change that enhanced women's and men's lives.

Education

If you think education is expensive, try ignorance.
Emma Goldman, feminist, anarchist

Creative minds have been known to survive any sort of bad training.
Anna Freud, psychiatrist

An investment in education brings enlightened commitment. The corridors of education provide access to skill, knowledge, and creativity. Pick and choose; doorways lead to learning. Academic choices open doors to occupational and career options. Cross thresholds and become immersed in new experiences and ideas. Author Ellen Metcalf characterized the importance of getting an education, "You have to recognize when the right place and the right time fuse and take advantage of that opportunity. There are plenty of opportunities out there. You can't sit back and wait." Education is powerful. It gives us the tools to improve life.

Linda Brown's father knew the importance of education, and he wanted the freedom to provide the best for his daughters. Mr. Brown's beliefs urged action. In the early 1950s, his third-grade daughter became the catalyst for the fight to end segregation in public schools. Assisted by the National Association for the Advancement of Colored People, and joined by other African American families, Linda Brown's father challenged the Topeka Board of Education after it denied Linda's enrollment in the nearby all-white elementary school. Thus began a national journey toward racial equality in education.

Linda Brown Thompson endures as a beacon of courage and excellence in education. She and her sister, Cheryl, co-founded the Brown Foundation for Educational Equity, Excellence and Research. The mission of this nonprofit organization is to build future leaders by developing, implementing, and supporting programs that invest in children. The Brown family's investment in education continues to yield benefits.

Women like Maria Mitchell, Ina Garten, and my Aunt Edith represent a talent for relational connection that promotes and encourages the excitement of learning. Social activists like Linda Brown and Maggie Kuhn shine with passion for learning and their belief in the power of education to rebalance inequities.

Education was not always an option for women. For centuries, women were considered mentally inferior and incapable of participation in the intellectual rigors of academic higher learning. Women persisted, knocking at and knocking down doors. Here is a sampling of some of their successes. Founded in 1833, Oberlin College was the first institution of higher education to accept women as students in the United States. In 1877, Helen Magill, a graduate student at Boston University, became the first American woman to earn a Ph.D. In 1945, the first woman was accepted to Harvard Medical School. In 1996 Virginia Military Institute accepted its first female students. Margaret Chase Smith, first woman to serve in both houses of Congress, confirmed part of women's persistence in pursuing access to higher education. "When people keep telling you that you can't do a thing, you kind of like to try it." Time may fly, but women's access to higher education travels step-by-hard-fought-step.

Medusa's story touches on women's freedom to tap into the power of education. Medusa, symbol of sovereign female wisdom, knows that while forbidden to women, knowledge is liberating. That girl had a good head on her shoulders. Just a little too late, Jean Kerr, playwright and humorist, warned, "If you can keep your head about you when all about you are losing theirs, it's just possible you haven't grasped the situation."

✺ Medusa ✺

Never born, she will always live.

Medusa represents the untamable intellectual power of women. Her snaky hairstyle symbolizes the electric whiz of ideas that race through her brain. Not fearful, but feared, this life-giving force of the feminine creative was decapitated in an act designed to silence the mental potential of all women. I imagine her voice on the power of women's intellect must have threatened somebody.

Medusa's ability to turn men to stone stands for the awe inspiring potential of women who pursue their educational goals and determination to improve their lives. Look carefully sometimes, you can spot the power of Medusa in university and college students, professors, deans, and presidents.

—From Greek mythology

Medusa underscored women's ambition to acquire knowledge. Her style, strength, and quest live on in bold, undefeated women everywhere. One little known fact: she coined the phrase, "having a bad hair day."

Jane Addams, founder of Hull House, put her own spin on conventional thinking about women's capabilities. "I do not believe that women are better than men. We have not wrecked railroads, nor corrupted legislatures, nor done many unholy things that men have done; but then we must remember that we have not had the chance."

The unenlightened considered the female brain relatively primitive and accepted that feminine creativity was best suited for the sustenance of homemaking, fertility, and child rearing. It was presumed that if women were educated, they would no longer wish to fulfill their traditional roles. Let women flit in the hallowed halls of academe, and they might sashay right past the rewarding joys of housework. Like, if women couldn't read, they would just spend all of their time cooking and cleaning.

Alas, this conventional kind of thinking has not entirely disappeared. Even though women outnumber men on today's college campuses, the notion that men have an innate superiority still lurks in some hearts and minds. Women continue to fight for equitable financial compensation, promising career opportunities, and educational leadership positions. Anglo-American author Phyllis Bottome stated, "There are two ways of meeting difficulties. You alter the difficulties or you alter yourself to meet them." Her words spell out a top-notch response to the obstacles women continue to encounter. Only I would say, do both: Engage education to strengthen your skills and expertise. Enlist creativity to eradicate barriers and take hold of opportunities. Switch on the high-voltage force of your creative feminine.

School

*It's a mistake to think that once you're done with school you need
never learn anything new.*
Sophia Loren, motion picture and stage actor

*Louie brought his girlfriend home and the nicest thing I can say
about her is, all her tattoos are spelled correctly.*
Dolly Parton as Truvy in Steel Magnolias

I have been in school for most of my life. As student, special
education teacher, learning difference consultant, administrator,
and university lecturer, I have immersed myself in the culture of
many institutions of learning. Here is my sense of schools at their
best. Schools are stimulating, safe, and intimate places to develop a
lifelong relationship with learning. They initiate us into the world
of creativity and prepare us to nurture and use our intelligence.
Vitalizing schools invite us to engage abilities, connect with others, and broaden perspectives. Schools empower students to construct personal meaning. They inspire visions beyond the shores
of today, stretching toward the future.

I try to keep that stuff in mind while I am teaching Creative
Process so that lectures are to the point, activities are meaningful,
self-assessments are thought-provoking, and interactions abound.
The three-hour class on experience, education, and learning starts
with students lining up in order of their happiest and most successful year in school starting from preschool to their current one.

I ask them to find a partner and tell each other the details of their choice. Later in the class, I ask them to write a letter to their favorite teacher telling them what it was that made a difference. My students begin to connect what I am saying about education with their own and other students' experiences. Together we create a learning community where ideas are shared.

Pulitzer Prize winning journalist and author Anna Quindlen wrote an essay in 1997 that illuminates the importance of teachers. She told the story of a teacher with a class of young children on a field trip to the zoo. She described the unrelenting attention that a teacher must commit to as she goes about getting her students there, keeping them safe, and, most importantly, "coming with twenty-three and going back to school with twenty-three." Quindlen shared her sense of awe at the dedication and hard work involved in teaching young minds the intricacies of numbers, letters, getting along, sharing, and taking us to the zoo and bringing us safely home.

Inspired teachers invest their talents in shaping schools and endowing the future. As the heart, soul, and brains of schools, they encourage learning with myriad approaches and are ever-searching for innovative ways to arouse creativity. With respect, they spark students' interest in the skills, information, and habits needed to create satisfying lives. Whether it is learning how to tie a shoelace, read a book, play the violin, ride a bike, conduct research, or solve problems in quantum physics, teachers kindle the joy of lifelong learning. Compelling schools are dynamic environments where teachers percolate with contagious creativity.

PAYOFF
Competence

If you want to partake of life, you have to grab a big fork
and dig in!
Anne Copeland, fiber arts appraiser, consultant

You don't have to worry. I've taken care of myself for a long time.
Holly Golightly in *Breakfast at Tiffany's*

Competence is the rock solid dividend earned as a result of education and experience. Proficiency is strengthened by learning and amplified by taking a chance. In an ever-altering world, love of learning pays off.

Adventures on the road ahead and maybe a few challenges— well, crank up your competence and get humming. Competence got cracking back in 1909 when Alice Huyler Ramsey left on her 3,800-mile, sixty-day, cross-country drive from New York to San Francisco. Alice was the first woman to drive an automobile across the United States. Traveling most of the journey without maps or paved highways and infrequent service stations, Ramsey's intrepid spirit and competence carried the day. This is how she put it. "I'll drive every inch of the way if it kills me." She made thirty more cross-country treks, was never in a traffic accident, and was named Woman Motorist of the Century in 1960.

Alice Ramsey said, "Good driving has nothing to do with sex. It's all above the collar." Her successful journey underscores learning's power to ramp up competence. Capability beguiles creativity to search for opportunities to extend skill and savoir faire. When faced with dicey decisions and untried hypotheses, competence reminds us of what we know, eliciting confidence that answers exist, puzzles unravel, and breakthroughs happen.

Pushing us beyond the familiar, competence nudges us to learn. Together, competence and creativity urge us to travel into new domains and test our mettle. Competent wild woman Peggy's life is a creative journey. Forever upbeat and positive, here's Peggy!

✑ Determination Pays Off ✑

An interview with a wild woman

Peggy's creative spirit is a well-organized combination of determination, practicality, and originality. As an incurable learner she's always game and loves a challenge. Peggy paints in oils, plays the piano, plays golf, rides horses, decorates and renovates homes, composes music, and writes books. She is a Renaissance woman.

Peggy experiences dilemmas as adventures and learning as opportunities rather than battles. Deeply felt spirituality emboldens her mental and emotional zest to explore alternate paths. Seriously creative and meticulously competent, Peggy earns success by concentration, thoroughness, and inspiration.

Peggy shines with the spirit of rosy outlooks and silver linings. Helen Keller, first deaf and blind person to earn a college degree, said, "No pessimist ever discovered the secrets of the stars, or sailed to an uncharted land, or opened a new heaven to the human spirit." I know Peggy would agree—two competent women and one hope-inspiring philosophy. They know from experience that competence bucks us up and spurs actions that augment potential and outwit adversity. What a return on an investment.

Ingenuity

You can do anything you want to do, if you know what to do.
Betty Carter, American jazz singer

However, one cannot put a quart in a pint cup.
Dorothy Perkins Gilman, writer, independent thinker

Ingenuity is the fast-track payoff of a stimulated brain that produces short cuts and on-the-spot answers. It has a knack for attention to details, notions, and hunches. The brainwork of ingenuity refreshes thinking and takes action.

Psst, we have a problem. That is all it takes. Ingenuity mobilizes learning and creativity. Scarlett O'Hara personifies the spirit of ingenuity. Scarlett's determination to achieve her goals is legendary, and her velvet-gloved, iron fist is a classic.

✑ Scarlett O'Hara ✑

Never born, she will always live.

Scarlett O'Hara loves Tara, her family's plantation. After the Civil War, the threat of losing Tara looms. Scarlett's taxes are due and she is without funds. Rhett Butler is the answer. She must look like an elegant million to ask for a loan, but she's been running the plantation and working in the fields. A sumptuous new frock is required. Where will she find what she needs and how will she ever pay for it? Scarlett's gaze sweeps the room. She spies her mother's green velvet portières. Ingenuity kicks in, and the rest is southern belle history.

—From *Gone With the Wind* created by Margaret Mitchell in the 1936 novel

Like Scarlett, ingenuity is ready for action. It scans our mental storehouse looking for information and ideas. Necessities, dilemmas, and uncertainties spark ingenious thinking and transform experience into creative pay dirt.

Learning adds to ingenuity's stockpile. Information and experience soup up ingenuity's fire power. Crafty ingenuity drives the unorthodox and races toward the unthinkable. My friend Regina has ingenuity down. No kidding! Outside dinner party, gate-crashing mosquitoes, old camping tent. Read on.

✑ One Bewitching Evening ✑

An interview with a wild woman

The setting was perfect. Candles, flowers, great food, superb conversation, and then—buzzzzzz—swarms of mosquitoes. We were ready to move inside when Regina remembered her easy-to-erect camping tent with mesh walls. "Pour another glass of wine. I'm sure I can pitch this tent in a flash." She could, and she did. Regina's ingenuity transformed itching into bewitching.

We all appreciate brilliant solutions. Feminist scholar and mystery writer Carolyn Heilbrun wrote, "Ideas move rapidly when their time comes." Occasionally outrageous, ingenuity uses the available, reinvents the old, and develops the new. Needs and problems succumb. That is part of ingenuity's charm. Author Marcelene Cox noted, "Life is like a camel; you can make it do anything except back up."

Wisdom

Never mistake knowledge for wisdom. One helps you make a living; the other helps you make a life.
Sandra Carey, writer

If you can't solve it, it's not a problem—it's reality.
Barbara Colorose, author

Wisdom is the premium return on a love-of-learning filled life. The dividend is paid in insight, practicality, and occasional wake-up calls. Wisdom accrues what is learned and intuited and offers unexpected solutions.

Athena, goddess of wisdom, was a fierce strategist. Informed and influential, she enlightened our understanding of creative thinking. Her wisdom recast and deepened the ways in which civilization understands creative power. Winning strategies and practical solutions were her specialty. Siding with the Greeks during the Trojan War, Athena contributed some wise-gal sagacity to the Trojan Horse ploy. I can hear her saying, "Let's give them a crackerjack gift, something with a surprise inside."

In Greek culture, Athena represents a classic view of wise women in action. Her wisdom combined knowledge, experience, insight, and haughty hubris. It guided her choices and judgment, and orchestrated her actions. Know-it-all dispenser of advice Lucy Van Pelt, revealed "I never made a mistake in my life. I thought I did once, but I was wrong." I think she has some Greek goddess irony and wisdom running in her veins.

Let me share some of my Mom's Irish-wise-woman perspective. She's like Athena, just exchange Irish prescience for haughty hubris. Athena loved her man, and Mom loved her three children. She tried to keep us safe and always moved quickly to heal our hurts and disappointments. Mom had an early warning system for danger that was almost infallible. If she said not to do something, I learned from experience that was 'nough said. I lost my front teeth jumping on a pogo stick that had gotten a thumbs-down rating from Mom. When disappointment or rejection struck, she moved in with unerring brilliant perspicacity. Whatever did or didn't happen, Mom believed that was the way it should be. Her words exactly: "If it's for you, it's for you. If you didn't get it, it was not for you." I am not sure if she was always accurate, but I still find comfort in Mom's wisdom.

Life infused with competence, ingenuity, and wisdom regenerates our passion and creativity. Wise women say live and learn, learn, learn! Court life's optimistic lessons. Take life in your arms and dance with the wise old moxie that outmaneuvers adversity, failure, and catastrophe. Here is wild woman wisdom straight from live-life-to-the-hilt Molly Ivins. "The first rule of holes: when you're in one, stop digging."

Chapter Six

Women
Achieve

They laughed at Joan of Arc, but she went right ahead and built it.

—Gracie Allen, movie, radio, and television comedian

When I started out, I didn't have any desire to be an actress or to learn how to act. I just wanted to be famous.

—Katharine Hepburn, Oscar Award-winning actor

omen sure can dazzle. Work commitments, family obligations, economic stability, social productivity, and personal fulfillment— women achieve it all. Happily we get to design and concoct our achievements. It is good to remember that work alone does not define us. Arm-in-arm with the feminine creative, we work, achieve, and play. Ah, the wonder of women as they manage the abundance of life.

We pursue the right to develop our talents and the opportunities to use them. Experience, expertise, and success invigorate women's efforts to choose where they will focus their creative energy. Women blaze trails as they explore options and invent opportunities. Marlene Dietrich explained women's savvy: "Darling, the legs aren't so beautiful, I just know what to do with them."

In pre–Bronze Age Crete, women played a pivotal role in all areas of life. They were civic leaders, administrators, artisans, and entrepreneurs, and they were priestesses in Crete's goddess-based religion. Cretan women participated in all sports, including bull leaping. Let me tell you about bull leaping. It consisted of a line of potential jumpers awaiting a charging bull. As the bull rushed headlong into the jumpers, each athlete, in turn, had to grab the horns of the bull and vault over to land feet first safely behind the bull. Yikes! And pray to the goddess.

In current times, and where else but sunny California, skateboarding wild women zoom on 8 x 30-inch thinly sliced boards of polypropylene that roll on small polyurethane wheels. The pros use a whole new vernacular of "kickflip indy grabs," "flat ground ollies," and "backside lipsides." Veteran female skaters notice that times are changing. Just a few years ago nobody wanted to watch a girl's contest, but audiences are getting bigger, and prize money is increasing.

Like female skateboarders, women have dreams and aspirations, and they too throw themselves into life with verve and velocity. Writer and lecturer Mary Lou Cook was on target when she wrote, " Creativity is inventing, experimenting, growing, taking risks, breaking rules, making mistakes, and having fun."

Yes, yes, I know that all women do not aspire to kickflip indy grabs, but we do want to use our talents to realize our potential. Creativity nudged me to make a career change a few years ago. In my own flat ground ollie, I left the familiar ground of family therapy and early childhood education to teach a university course on creative process and write this book about women and creativity. For my next trick—I don't know. Yet!

Creative women follow a personal compass, letting it guide their intuitive sense of direction. Each creator's beliefs about success influence her choices. Mary and I did not know each other when we sat together at a luncheon lecture. As we chit-chatted, I learned that Mary was a visual artist with a special interest in writing and illustrating children's books. She learned that I was in the process of interviewing women for this book. Coincidence or the rhythm of creativity? By the end of the lecture, we had a date set for an interview at her studio.

✑ Flying Colors ✑

An interview with a wild woman

Mary has always been an artist. But it was while she was reading bedtime stories to her young son that a new path for her talent emerged. As Mary read to her young son, she watched his response to the stories and their illustrations. She learned to appreciate the power of children's books. It was the shapes and colors in the illustrations that attracted his rapt attention and roused his excitement most.

Saturated hues and tinted pastels flow from Mary's paintbrush. Artistry and pigment are set free. Mary's magic creates caravans of colorful characters and scenery that weave into children's storybooks. Mary imbues ordinary paper with wonder-working images. Her talent and hard work create delight for her young readers.

Creative women want to make a difference. Culinary goddess Julia Child certainly did. Cooking changed Julia's life: "I was thirty-two when I started cooking; up until then, I just ate." As a celebrity chef, she familiarized American audiences with French cuisine and cooking techniques, transforming how we cook and eat. Child's cookbooks and television shows reflected her infatuation with the art of preparing food and her appetite for enjoying superb meals. Julia Child was at home in a kitchen; Georgia O'Keeffe was at home anywhere she could paint. She captured brilliance in flowers, bones, and landscapes that only her eyes could see and only her brush-strokes could reveal. O'Keeffe disclosed, "I hate flowers—I paint them because they are cheaper than models and they don't move." She never painted a person in all of her documented works.

Julia's and Georgia's ambitions animated enterprises. Their passion-filled work and their career exploits nourished our senses. Women like Julia Child and Georgia O'Keeffe are models for all of us wild women who redefine what it is to be a wise woman who pursues and attains what she wants.

WORK

My family can always tell when I'm well into a novel because the meals get very crummy.
Anne Tyler, American novelist

Housekeeping is like being caught in a revolving door.
Marcelene Cox, writer

Women have worked, will work, are working. Our work is essential, embedded in life. Women succeed by tackling tasks at hand and getting the jobs done. Creative women display versatility and flexibility when prioritizing, innovating, and reframing daily tasks and career paths.

Life can feel like a high-wire act: never falter, trust your team, and keep moving. Imbalance is a part of life, impassioning and energizing our efforts. Women master the impossible, feed the pet, win the man, have babies, cook dinner, and make sure no one runs out of toilet paper. Helen Kreis Wallenda balanced in the air with the greatest of ease and never used a net. Helen was only seventeen when she first climbed up on her husband's shoulders. With dare-devil elegance she became the point on the family's crowning achievement, the seven-person pyramid. Helen balanced on top of two aerialists, who were supported by four aerialists. As one unit, they all moved across a high wire twenty-five feet above the circus floor. Helen said, "We live to entertain and thrill those who are circus-oriented."

Day-to-day feats can feel like circus routines. Taming lions, spinning plates, shooting out of cannons, and, no surprise, twenty-five clowns tumbling from a miniscule car describes some days. Stuff gets dropped, and there is a lot of clean-up. Practice and hard work make it look simple. That is the artistry and serious business of the creative feminine. Like American author Louisa May Alcott wrote, "Housekeeping ain't no joke." But then Bristish journalist Katherine Whitehorn made me laugh with this: "When it comes to housework the one thing no book of household management can ever tell you is how to begin. Or maybe I mean why."

Historically, women's work centered on the home. Tradition purports that men leave home to do real work and women stay home to clean and take care of kids. This conventional, handed-down notion is limiting. Narrow expectations dampen aspiration, hinder development, and curtail choice. What does that do to creativity? Wait, wait, don't tell me. These limitations dilute the very spirit of creativity and sap its energy. Author Katherine Mansfield wrote, "Risk! Risk anything! Care no more for the opinion of others, for those voices. Do the hardest thing on earth for you. Act for yourself. Face the truth!"

Work that is considered women's domain is indispensable. Women preserve life, home, and spirit. We create new life, nurture those who are sick or injured, and confront those who threaten our family. American actor Sarah Brown writes what women intuitively know: "The only thing that ever sat its way to success was a hen." Women's household endeavors on behalf of their families often exist unapplauded and unpaid, totally expected, and absolutely relied upon. Housework and child care become invisible as work when they are masked as a natural, inherently female display of love and nest building.

Most women will be employed outside the home at some time in their lives. Nevertheless, the main weight of caring for households, children, and aging parents still falls primarily on women, whether working outside of the home or not. Work is not all that life offers. American psychiatrist Jean Baker Miller wrote, "Most so-called women's work is not recognized as real activity. One reason for this attitude may be that such work is usually associated with helping others' development rather than self-enhancement or self-employment." Child care, cooking, cleaning, and general homemaking are still assigned to women, even when someone else is hired to do them.

Working hones judgment and increases capabilities. Partners, children, employers, customers, patients, and employees crucially shape what we wish for and require. Nancy Coey, healthcare author and lecturer, explained work's synergy this way. "When work, commitment, and pleasure all become one, and you reach that deep well where passion lives, nothing is impossible." A creative work culture generates and executes innovative solutions. It is a context that merges creative energy with talents, ideas, and passions.

Anais Nin, diarist and author, encouraged women, "How wrong is it for a woman to expect the man to build the world she wants, rather than to create it herself." Work enables us to fulfill dreams, meet needs, and invigorate creativity. More than means to a financial end or a foe to be vanquished, work is an opportunity to apply what we know and to learn new stuff. Work that we love is an immersion in an atmosphere that eggs on creativity. At its best, work offers the experience of making a contribution, responding to challenge, providing for ourselves, and supporting others. Plunge Jane Tennison's creativity into criminal-infested waters and it thrives.

Detective Superintendent Jane Tennison

Never born, she will always live.

Jane Tennison's work is her life. Her battle-fatigued but undaunted commitment pushes her to find murderers, blackmailers, and torturers while her compassion urges her to seek justice for victims and their families. Jane's ingenuity, determination, and courage solve the case, and she does not mind in the least rattling a few cages to get the job done.

Detective Superintendent Tennison's in-your-face leadership style keeps her in the administrative hot seat. Ambitious, tough, and bold, she unflinchingly confronts old-boy police patriarchy with down and dirty challenges. Integrity and ball-busting hard work keep her in the job as well as on the job.

—From *Prime Suspect*, a crime drama series, created by Linda LaPlante in 1992

Jane never seems to question her chosen path; it is her work, and she owns the job. After seeing this career-driven dynamo bounce back from defiant team members, resistant bosses, and aggressive villains, I feel my resolve firm and gusto surge. Tennison's self-confidence, decision making, and work ethic inspire me to stick with it—whatever "it" happens to be.

The meaning of work changes with time, but its importance remains a constant. Former superintendent of U.S. Army nurses Dorothea Dix believed that, "In a world where there is so much to be done, I felt strongly impressed that there must be something for me to do." Giving us a different slant on the relevance of work, Anglo-Irish writer Dorothy Leigh Sayers surmised, "A human being must have an occupation if he or she is not to become a nuisance to the world."

Work and creativity unfold throughout life. The focus of our energy mirrors changes in our bodies, families, and careers. Life extends and creativity elaborates. Here is the short form. Young women invest creative talent into developing friends and mentors, finding committed partners, and securing education and career. With those in good working order, women center on nurturing children, expanding careers, and multiplying roles. As women mature, their attention shifts to taming emotional stressors and accommodating physical and hormonal changes. Mid-life women typically provide the support for aging parents and returning children and grandchildren. In later life women can focus on themselves, seeking mental challenge, physical health, and emotional vitality. Frances Lear, founder of *Lear's Magazine*, was even briefer when she wrote, "I believe that the second half of one's life is meant to be better than the first half. The first half is finding out how you do it. And the second half is enjoying it." Wild woman Rena got an early career start and is sharing her wisdom and insight as she moves into ever-evolving next phases.

✎ Inner Voice ❧

An interview with a wild woman

When Rena was six years old, she started her own newspaper. She has always had insight about her passions and the inspiration to follow them. As a journalism pioneer, Rena plunged into the driving, competitive, and scarcely-a-woman-to-be-seen newspaper environment. To sustain and nurture her creative feminine, she began to meet with other female trailblazers. Together they encouraged each other to use and extend their talents. Rena quips, "Being a woman is fun, if you do it right."

Filled with luminous energy and creativity, Rena says, "Everyday is a blank slate; figure out what to do with it." Rena's three books capture the thinking of women who want to be productive, use their talents, and make the world better. As a researcher, wild woman Rena delves to find answers. The results of her work arm us with information about the ways real women explore their spirituality and make life enhancing decisions.

So how did Venus de Milo lose her arms? Was she conducting a symphony orchestra or washing dishes? Passion underwrites our achievements. Women have an enormous capacity for creativity, and we hunger to know that our lives and our work matter. Supportive contexts multiply the benefits by nurturing self-confidence, encouraging determination, valuing diversity, and rewarding the use of creativity.

CAREER

I have yet to hear a man ask for advice on how to combine marriage and a career.
Gloria Steinem, co-founder of *Ms. Magazine*

Nobody objects to a woman being a good writer or sculptor or geneticist if, at the same time, she manages to be a good wife, good mother, good looking, good tempered, well groomed and unaggressive.
Leslie McIntyre, author

When women build careers and gain positions of power, they extend other women's opportunities for education, training, jobs, and careers. Less than thirty years ago, young women were guided into traditionally female jobs. Women were thought best suited to be teachers, nurses, and secretaries, not doctors, architects, or politicians. Most girls were not aware of the full range of career possibilities. Today, women join the work force in more fields and embrace a wider range of career options.

When research showed that adolescent girls were receiving very little career information and encouragement, the Ms. Foundation did something. In 1993, they designated a national day to take daughters to work. The intention was to expose girls to the world of work and expand their ideas about the range of possible careers. The popularity of the concept sparked interest for boys as well. So Take Our Daughters to Work® Day is now Take Our Daughters and Sons to Work® Day. Changing the name and the focus—good idea or not?

Creative women help young girls expand their knowledge of the working world when they share their work world wisdom. Telling what they do, what they love, and the preparation required puts muscle on understanding's skeleton. What do you want to be when you grow up? Answers come from self-awareness influenced by what is seen, heard, and experienced. Entry-level jobs and volunteer experiences assist in establishing a sense of the working self. These first working-world encounters initiate career ideas and open doors to interests that may become passions.

Air Force Lt. Col. Eileen Collins, first female space shuttle commander, shared this piece of family–influencing–career–perspective. "My daughter just thinks that all moms fly the space shuttle." In fact, it is our family that introduces first tastes of career exploration. Work ethic and careers are influenced by school and community experiences and media messages. Each generation develops ways to connect education and work that support participation in family and career.

Ultimate role model Oprah Winfrey proclaimed her source of inspiration. "For every one of us that succeeds, it's because there's somebody there to show you the way out. The light doesn't always necessarily have to be in your family; for me it was teachers and school." Wild woman Elba's inspiration started with her family. Elba believes in the power of community spirit and the importance of nurturing the upcoming generation. Springing from her fun-loving, hard-working ethos, Elba's commitment to family and community is super-charged with achievement.

❧ Role Model Power ❧

An interview with a wild woman

Elba shares how she made the choice to become a pediatric dentist. "With three generations of doctors in the family, I knew early on that I would follow that path." Elba was always interested in directly affecting people's lives. She combines her love of children with her meticulous attention to detail and readiness to work hard. Young patients and their parents are in good hands with gentle and conscientious Dr. Garcia.

As an elected public servant, city councilwoman Elba says, "The world is our neighborhood; we must provide opportunities for people to use their talents to make things better." With unlimited energy, Elba sees the needs in the community, is ready for hard work, and knows there is always more to do. Arts, education, minorities, and health are the issues and needs that remain at the top of her agenda.

"If a young woman sees me doing something, she will say, 'If Elba can do it, I can do it.'" Elba understands that role models carry a responsibility to those who aspire to improve their lives. With her dedicated work ethic and special brand of charisma, Elba opens the eyes of others to worlds of possibilities. Elba, professional, homemaker, community leader, and volunteer, says, "Lead by example." And girl, does she ever!

Economic opportunities, parental and school guidance, coincidence, and luck are a part of the way careers are selected. Values, inner longings, talents, interests, and livable incomes influence choices. Decisions are shaped by role models, mentors, educational and occupational aspirations, and willingness to modify family roles to accommodate career, achievement, and connections.

Sandra Day O'Connor's career choice made history. Of the 110 Supreme Court Justices nominated by a President and approved by the Senate, only two have been women. That is less than two percent. The first Justice was appointed in 1798; Sandra Day O'Connor, the first woman Justice, was appointed in 1981. That is more than 180 years. Oyez.

As a young girl, Sandra Day rode horses, roped cows, repaired fences, and shot guns. As a new-to-the-bar lawyer in Arizona, Sandra Day O'Connor discovered that local law firms would not hire a woman. Her response was to start her own law firm. These experiences paid off in her job as Supreme Court Justice. In the Supreme Court, O'Connor tamed tough compromises and blazed trails for women. In retirement she looks to the future. Rather than quietly settling into private life, her schedule is filled with appeals court hearings, lectures, and book writing. O'Connor lives by the motto, "Maybe in error, but never in doubt."

A lack of family and mentor support, plus a meager fund of role models and options, narrows perspective and diminishes alternatives. I wonder if poet and essayist Audre Lorde had looked into

Bonnie Parker's soul when she wrote, "If I didn't define myself for myself, I would be crunched into other people's fantasies for me and eaten alive."

Bonnie Parker made decisions and made history, too. I guess even bad girls have career paths. As a young woman, Bonnie's biggest dream was to escape her humdrum life. She had a flair for theatrics and a love of adventure. In high school, she was usually on the honor roll, excelled in creative writing, and demonstrated talent in the dramatic arts. Parker's unique career path entwined her life with a bank robbing murderer. Excitement and drama were played out with tommy guns, ambushes, shootouts, car chases, and romance.

Using her high school talents to feed the media with on-the-scene snapshots and biographical poems, Bonnie created misunderstood-desperados-in-star-crossed-love images. The Barrow Gang had a pistol-packing, camera-snapping public relations gal. True to her lifelong love for sensational commotion, Bonnie and her lover died in a hail of bullets. Words from one of Bonnie's poems are etched on her tombstone: "As the flowers are all made sweeter by the sunshine and the dew, so this old world is made brighter by the lives of folks like you." More than 20,000 people came to Bonnie Parker's funeral. Bonnie would have liked that.

I am glad we no longer need to go out in a spray of bullets to adapt careers and employment to encompass our needs and desires. Traditional, non-traditional, and entrepreneurial women are on the move, taking responsibility for their progress through life. American aerospace pioneer Ruth Bancroft Law hard sells women's wide-ranging career capabilities. "There is a world-old controversy that crops up whenever women attempt to enter a new field. Is a woman fit for that work? It would seem that a woman's success in any particular field would prove her fitness for that work, without regard to theories to the contrary."

Emma Peel inspires me with her power, brains, and flawless manners, and she never, ever plays the damsel in distress. Emma has a clear sense of herself and a partner who thrives on her independence. Physical strength, intelligence, and nifty clothes. As I watch Mrs. Peel, I definitely make notes.

✍ Emma Peel ✍

Never born, she will always live.

Mrs. Peel is a force to be reckoned with. In hand-to-hand combat, Emma is formidable. Fearlessly cool, her physical strength and prowess are matched by her wit and charm. Emma drives fast cars, karate chops villains, figures out arcane clues, and always bags evil-doers. Mentally brilliant and tough as titanium, she is ready for action in an instant. Her cohort in adventure, John Steed, has only to say, "Mrs. Peel, we're needed."

—From *The Avengers*, a quirky spy series, created by Sydney Newman in 1961

If the door is barred, Emma Peel kicks it in. Women are opening career doors, but not exactly in Mrs. Peel's style. Instead of karate chops, women use brains and energy. Their practices bring clarity to making choices, balancing rewards and costs, mastering workplace politics, and improving job options. Today's female heroes ignite the notion that the working world must acknowledge and accommodate women's participation in equal partnership.

Career, work, and family require adjustment and accommodation. Golda Meir, former prime minister of Israel, explained a dilemma many women wrestle with: "At work, you think of the children you have left at home. At home, you think of the work you've left unfinished. Such a struggle is unleashed within yourself. Your heart is rent." Armed with the strength of their creative feminine, women use resources and constraints to produce refined and workable outcomes. Women work at home, combine work with marriage or children, or re-enter a career when divorced or empty-nested. Thank goodness creativity is a renewable energy source. Choices and decisions open new routes to successful and fulfilling lives at work and at home.

Author Jane Sellman wrote, "The phrase 'working mother' is redundant." I think Terri would agree. Her career is going great guns, she is an awesome community volunteer, and she has two, all-star, soccer-playing adolescents. As tactical commanders, genius organizers, and dedicated parents, Terri and her husband, Tim, are equal partners in supporting their thriving family. Creativity rides shotgun with Terri, the ultimate wild woman carpooler.

The SUV Backs Out of the Driveway and...

An interview with a wild woman

Soccer season is a time for small miracles. Terri knows five different routes for any individual carpool itinerary and can be in two different places at the same moment. She adapts to the world as it is, here and now. "Mothers have to be creative to work things out for their children."

The season may be tough, but Terri is tougher. SUVs pull up, horns toot, doors open, and athletes hop in or out. She keeps track of snacks, changes of clothes, required equipment, cell phone numbers, addresses, and the location of myriad playing fields. Did I mention schedules? There are practice schedules, game schedules, competition schedules, and season schedules.

Terri is committed to providing life-enhancing experiences and adventures for her children. She is a crackerjack connector and facilitator; she focuses on team success and enjoys being a cheerleader for others. Family, home, church, work, and neighborhood; her arms embrace them all. "What we create begins as a game plan, to be executed and adjusted as we move toward success."

I asked Terri where she got her inspiration. In a heartbeat, Terri says, "I've always admired and been inspired by my mom. She is a courageous life force who makes the tough decisions and speaks her mind." Journalist, author, and my all-time favorite feminist, Gloria Steinem, framed it this way, "Without leaps of imagination, or dreaming, we lose the excitement of possibilities. Dreaming, after all, is a form of planning."

Career paths can be circuitous. So where to obtain career advice? British journalist Katherine Whitehorn opined, "The best career advice given to the young is: find out what you like doing best and get someone to pay you for doing it." The rhythms and routines of careers mimic those of life. Careers develop over time with quirky recursions, plateaus, and growth spurts and unfold in opportunities, steps, and stages. Creativity shapes career paths with ambition, competition, and cooperation. It intrigues and maneuvers on our behalf, generating possibilities. Careers can offer new experiences, flexibility, and independence.

PLAY

If I get to pick what I want to do, then it's play; if someone tells me that I have to do it, then it's work.
Patricia Nourot, author, professor of early childhood development

The world is your playground. Why aren't you playing?
Ellie Katz, author

Fun occurs in the present. Watch what happens when two children meet and one says to the other, "Ya wanna play?" My heart beats faster just writing that.

Play elicits creativity. Play gives us new ideas and flaunts restrictive rules. So, play the fool, play up, play around, play down, play by ear, or play possum. Choose one or all of the above, but please play. Wild woman Pat combines a sense of play with versatile musical talent and beguiles audiences to join in her wonderful sense of the absurd.

✌ Hats Off ✍

An interview with a wild woman

Thirty years ago, Pat sat at a piano and sang a few songs. That's how it all got started. Then, humor and creativity wove a little play into the performance. Ad-libbing, she grabbed a few hats and stuck them on her head as she pounded the keyboard. *Spanish Eyes* meant a sombrero, *I Fall to Pieces*, called forth a hat with Humpty Dumpty on top— you get the idea.

The audience has fun, and Pat is a hoot. The side-splitting laughter and rib-tickling silliness are contagious. New venues welcomed her, and new hats piled high. "Comedy Tonight" is a thriving event with raucously cross-pollinated hats and songs. Number of performances: current count, close to 2,000. Number of hats: current count, close to one hundred.

Play invites a smile and encourages harmonious interactions. Pat says, "If you want to look good, get with someone who's really good." Playing around and having fun with Pat makes you look really good.

When asked how I play, I was stumped. I have fun with every-thing. If there was an Olympic event for playing, I would be a gold medal contender. No kidding! I have fun cooking, gardening, ham-mering, sanding, and just about anything that gets me sweaty and dirty. I love to play with clothes, get dressed up, go out with friends, have parties, and eat out. Traveling, getting lost, and hav-ing adventures are high on my list of playtime possibilities. I have fun staying home, reading, and watching old movies. Some of my best play time is wrapped up in my merrily-rolling-along marriage. My husband Kent and I play well together. Lastly, I have fun tickling people who want more playfulness in their lives.

In a twinkle, play transforms reality, the larger context that holds all we do. "Play exists for its own sake," Episcopal priest, spiri-tual director, and author Margaret Guenther said, "Play is for the moment; it is not hurried, even when the pace is fast and timing seems important. When we play, we also celebrate holy useless-ness. Like the calf frolicking in the meadow, we need no pretense or excuse. Work is productive; play, in its disinterestedness and self-forgetting, can be fruitful." In league with creativity, play animates life and inspires total immersion. Play can suspend the passage of time and move us beyond responsibility's reach.

World-class redhead Katharine Hepburn piped in her perfect Connecticut Yankee accent, "If you obey all the rules, you miss all the fun." Hepburn personified strong independent women with minds of their own. Jazz Age flapper Zelda Sayre Fitzgerald went further—she wrote and broke her own rules. This Alabama-born wild woman did not ride in taxis; she rode on them. She flaunted convention, explored and expressed her numerous talents, and flirted outrageously with life.

At age eleven, Zelda Sayre already knew that what she liked to do best was to play. Drawing and painting came in second and third. Consistent with her young girl preferences, as an adult she described her ideal day as starting with a peach for breakfast followed by golf and a swim; her perfect career was being either a writer or a dancer.

Zelda's unquenchable desire to be an artist was demonstrated in writing, dancing, and painting. Zelda wrote one novel, many short stories, and magazine and newspaper articles. She pursued her passion for dance by taking lessons from several famous ballet teachers. Zelda captured whimsy, imagination, and fantasy in her work as a painter. Her embellished photographs, fanciful doll houses, and historically accurate paper dolls were products of Zelda having fun.

Play provided impetus for Zelda's creativity and stability in a chaotic life. She played with words, images, and ideas integrating them in her very own Zelda style. "You took what you wanted from life, if you could get it, and you did without the rest," Zelda said. She always remained true to her fun-loving sense of play.

Play is serious business. A sprinkle of fun can relieve pressure and help us cope with raging feelings and appalling provocations. Fun-loving involvement keeps us physically and mentally fit. Play supercharges well-being. Play assists us as we manage demanding emotions and experiences by creating easy-going responses. JoAnna Brandi, customer care coach and author, ballyhooed the playful approach. "Sometimes you just have to be absurd. Nothing stifles creativity like routine rationality." Play, on a mission, keeps people functional during times of stress.

Enjoyment and recreation entice creative spontaneity. Summoning the wonder and freshness of first times, play ignites passion and reconnects dots. Play discovers the unexpected and unpredictable.

Play imbues creative work with energy, enthusiasm, satisfaction, and meaning. Play takes on drudgery and makes fun of it. Wild woman and violin whiz Jennifer plays to a perfect pitch. I have known Jennifer since she was in kindergarten, and even then she impishly explored her creativity and played her violin like an angel. Here are a few adult Jennifer moments.

∽ Fun, Talent, and Play That Violin ∾

An interview with a wild woman

In a White Christmas *à la* Jennifer, she hung swathes of white satin over walls and furniture. White wine, vanilla ice cream, white truffles, and Brie were on the menu. With playful humor and a passion for whimsy, Jennifer filled her tiny apartment with close to a hundred friends. The theme was winter white, and everything was!

The inception and production of Jennifer's CD, *Violin-land*, involved lots of people and took a year to complete. Jennifer entwined ambition, fantasy, and superlative violin playing to form an ingeniously crafted project. Jennifer says, "I know it's a solid piece of work." She creates play-filled enterprises that capture and mobilize her friends, as well as innocent bystanders. Floating in the music of *Violinland* fills my imagination with clouds of melodious lyrics.

Open Mike, a live show where artists are invited or sign up to perform, is a perfect venue for Jennifer. Her playful stage persona and her skillful violin playing combine to produce breathtaking performances. "I like to be excited by my performance and evoke something in the audience. I remember those." When Jennifer plays, she gets standing ovations. Connections occur between Jennifer and her audiences that transcend music and performance.

Play influences who we are, what we do, and who we become. As May-lin Soong, aka Madame Chiang Kai-shek, Chinese educator, reformer, and politician, said, "We become what we do." We role-play, discover and recover gifts and talents. Playing dress-up, playing house, playing star reporter, and playing wildly emoting diva are some of my personal favorites. Play stars in achievement's comedies and dramas. It plays a potent role in survival and success. Drawing on the powers of imagination and spontaneity, a sense of play makes it easy and fun to perfect abilities.

In mirthful communication with heart, soul, spirit, and hulla-baloo, play stimulates happiness and well being. Play is a powerful catalyst, pumping juicy life into what we do. It cavorts along with us on exhilarating adventures. Lucia Capacchione, art therapist and author, summarized the gravity of play, "Play keeps us vital and alive. It gives us an enthusiasm for life that is irreplaceable. Without it, life just doesn't taste good." Work, careers, and a life filled with a playful spirit. What could be better? I cannot think of a thing.

Chapter Seven

Women Lead

The only safe ship in a storm is leadership.

—Faye Wattleton, equality for women activist

So, where's the Cannes Film Festival being held this year?

—Christina Aguilera, American vocalist

We all get to lead sometime. Leaders influence, motivate, empower, and are needed whenever individuals come together with a common intent. Whether leading a family, community group, business, organization, or country, leaders are most effective when they build consensus and encourage collaboration.

As leaders, women really and truly pay attention. We keep our fingers on the pulse of those who follow. People, places, and social interactions carry critical information. Text and subtext contain meaning-filled messages. Women know this so we tune into people and plug into context. We read faces, translate tones of voice, and interpret body language. Indirect communication is essential as we seek understanding, conflict resolution, and a shared vision.

Women's leadership encompasses the capacity to nurture others and encourage collaborative achievement. We say invest in relationships, share interests, and contribute to personal causes and beliefs. Canadian author Margaret Atwood said, "We still think of a man as a born leader and a powerful woman as an anomaly." With the emerging creative feminine in modern society, that way of thinking is fading fast. As a shining example of women's leadership, the Reverend Diane is a wild woman leader who glows with the spirit of her creative feminine.

⚮ Impossible . . . Not a Possibility! ⚮

An interview with a wild woman

Diane is the leader of a one hundred-year-old inner-city, United Methodist church. When she became pastor, the church was experiencing financial challenges, facility disrepair, and a dwindling congregation. Diane and her creative feminine confronted these impossibilities with faith, passion, and hard work.

Who knows what is possible? Diane believes that she and the church are there to serve the community in a respectful, affirming, and supportive partnership. Her leadership style is burlap strong, and her faith is pure grit. She says, "I can mobilize people into joyous transformations." And she does.

Diane breaks some rules and waylays a few sacred cows. She is a master of improvisation and an instigator of unlikely teams. To address the financial challenges, she borrowed money, renovated and rented space, sought out new partners, tore down fences, and prayed. Early successes included: collaborations with a charter school, an after-school program, another church's congregation, and a day-care center. All became paying tenants at the church.

Diane had a dream. People were abandoning her church. Next morning she began the practice of walking the neighborhood, knocking on doors, and inviting folks to nurture their spiritual life. She said, "Please come to church . . . to services, to work, to share, and to nourish and sustain the human community." The community responded. Volunteers keep the food pantry going, the building in repair, and the garden thriving. The church hosts Amigo Days, an annual, community event that joins church and neighbors in repairing homes and urban churches. Diane versus Impossible—smart money is on Diane.

Diane's faith and leadership have created situations that foster commitment and rebuilt a vital community resource. Diane's story illustrates women's creative responses to the responsibilities of leadership. As a creative force, she does not just talk, she leads by example and inspires others to achieve. Women like Diane offer service, talent, and time, and they establish and maintain relationships. We encourage collective success, the essence of leadership.

Do not think for a minute that women's relationship-based leadership is wimpy. Oh, no! When women embrace their creative power, certainty is challenged and setbacks can be obliterated or recognized as opportunity for growth. With creativity aglow, women recognize obstacles and refuse to be limited by them. Margaret Thatcher once said, "No woman will become prime minister of the UK." Then she went on to become the first female prime minister in her country. As a creative woman, be willing to surprise yourself and exceed your own expectations. As leaders, women rock and rule, yeah!

She never had a paying job, a high profile career, or served in an elected office, but Rose Fitzgerald Kennedy was a rock solid leader. Never underestimate the power of her creative feminine in leading her children and living a life of faith, dedication, and responsible action. Daughter, wife, mother, and matriarch were a few of her roles. Her Irish-Catholic and political values were always evident. Rose Kennedy lived her life in covenant with her stated beliefs.

Leadership in motherhood, as created by Rose Kennedy, played out this way. Raising a family of nine is a big job. Her expectations were simple: study, do your best, and stay close to your family. Rose kept order by pinning to-do notes on herself and keeping index cards on each of her children.

Rose Kennedy endured tragedy and celebrated accomplishment. She led by example as she coped with one daughter's intellectual disability and applauded as another daughter founded the Special Olympics. We saw her share joy with three of her sons as they achieved political success. We learned the depth of her Catholic faith as she mourned the loss of four adult children.

A tradition of public service and a love of politics flowed in her Irish blood. She passed along those passions. Many of Rose Fitzgerald Kennedy's progeny are writers, activists, politicians, and lawyers. Her belief that with great privileges come great responsibilities inspired a family that dedicates itself to making the world a better and at times more interesting place. Their contributions to humanity continue. Until her death, at age 105, Rose Fitzgerald walked a path of family unity and public service and built a legacy of leadership through example and dedication.

As leaders, women make friends, share interests, and contribute to personal causes and beliefs. Their successful leadership enriches families, improves communities, and strengthens social connectedness. Actor and world-class dancer Vera-Ellen said succinctly, "Getting involved is so, so … involving." When Elizabeth philosophizes on the topic of creative leadership she has a lot more than that to say. She is full of energy, wit, and a joy for life that you can spot a mile away. Elizabeth's leadership moxie travels at warp speed. The minute you meet this community volunteer you know she is a wild woman.

✎ Mischievous Joy ✎

An interview with a wild woman

Things get interesting the moment Elizabeth starts talking. She plunges into detailed anecdotes related to her life as a homemaker, wife, mother, and grandmother. She pours her willingness to learn and break patterns into her work as a community volunteer, mentor, and church deacon.

Elizabeth's philosophy of life is to stay interested, interesting, productive, and engaged. She says, "If goals are narrow, your world diminishes." No shrinking world for Elizabeth. Her strategy is: be prepared to fail, but have plan B, C, or D ready to harness.

How does Elizabeth act on her convictions? One of the many ways is by mentoring women getting out of jail.

Her support and example open doors for women who are hungry for new perspectives and options. Who better? Elizabeth is a dynamic public speaker. Her topic is building self-confidence skills. No big surprise!

Elizabeth is contagiously joyous and outstanding in the fun department. She says her outlook is a result of a deep-seated sense of humor. For example, as the only woman on a board of directors, Elizabeth's response was, "If you don't get another woman on this board, I'm going to picket." Retelling the anecdote, eyes sparkling with mischief, she concludes by saying, ". . . and more women became board members."

She admits to a few failures. She tells about a time she thought a contrasting color lattice work would be interesting on the bedroom walls. No one slept soundly until the jarring diamond pattern was taken down. Peppered with energetic humor, she describes going down in roaring flames with all flags flying . . . as the only way to go.

Elizabeth leads and creates her way. Just because all women are female, by no means indicates a cookie-cutter pattern. Individuality, wide-ranging viewpoints, traditions, and modes of expression bring beauty and strength to the creative feminine. United States diplomat Jeane Kirkpatrick elucidated, "Look, I don't even agree with myself at times." Generations of women have influenced our ideas about responsible leadership. Potent leaders have some traits in common, but they transcend typecasting. They swim in pools of diversity in perspectives, interests, insights, and knowledge.

Women's innovative variations reward accomplishment, respect effort, and nurture ability. We choose to lead in order to benefit others and create change. Leadership, done female style, nurtures mutuality, potential, and growth. Women encourage working together for desired results, achieved collectively. Courageous leaders recognize that leadership is not a discrete attribute but a bold commitment that juices up energy, gives meaning to efforts, and leads to a better future. American cultural anthropologist Ruth Benedict related, "I long to speak out the intense inspiration that comes to me from the lives of strong women." As leaders, women inspire vision, connection, courage, and commitment.

VISION: ACTIVISTS

I do not think that I could ever really love a woman who had not,

for one reason or another, been upon a broomstick.

Karen Blixen, Danish writer who had a farm in Africa

To me, success means effectiveness in the world, that I am able

to carry my ideas and values into the world—that I am able to

change it in positive ways.

Maxine Hong Kingston, writer, academic

Yep, vision is what you see, and how you see it. Is that all? Nope, vision contains desire, hope, and insight. Visionary leadership, female style, conjures images that stimulate connection and momentum. We know to hold the dream in view, build on strengths, respect values, and encourage success.

Keen-sighted women leaders see the strength in team members working together to inspire others. They recognize the paths that transform intention and conviction into cohesive efforts and affirming payoffs. Girls, stick to your leadership guns. The world needs the balancing effect of feminine energy.

Forward thinking activists discern the need for change. They do not hesitate to plead and argue their platform for change. Their efforts transform protest into policy. These conduits for change rouse political, civic, and social institutions to action-changing policies, laws, practices, and regulations. And, hooray, they influence funding, too. Productive activists awaken compassion while standing against destruction, exclusion, and poverty of spirit. What a boon to our heritage of bounty, altruism, and equality. Read on for examples of activism spiced with the creative feminine.

As activists, women model determination to direct their own lives, exist with safety, and prevail with satisfaction. Motivated by a vision of a just world for all, activists dare to be courageous. Let me tell you about one such historical wild woman.

Mother Jones was once called "the most dangerous woman in America." After losing her husband and all four children during the 1867 yellow fever epidemic, and all of her property in the

1871 Chicago fire, Mary Harris Jones was forced to fend for herself. She experienced low wages, long hours, and unsafe work environments. An American labor activist was born.

Mary Harris Jones's talents as organizer, orator, and writer involved her in the heart of the labor movement. With wit, words, and courage, she battled full-tilt against poverty and powerlessness. Once, she organized a children's march to underscore the hideous evils of child labor. The protest ended in front of President Theodore Roosevelt's house with the young participants waving banners emblazoned with "We want time to play" and "We want to go to school." Through strikes, marches, and rallies in mining camps, railroad towns, and textile factories, Mother Jones's mission was to improve life for workers and their families.

Much like Mother Jones, other fiercely persuasive female activists strive to impel improvement in the universe. As proponents of human rights and dignity, they espouse protection from harm and escape from violence and abuse. As defenders, they galvanize the rights of inclusion and participation in the mainstream. They urge respect for choice and equitable access to resources.

Two movies and two Oscar-winning stars portrayed powerful, real-life activists who effected positive change for all people.

Norma Rae tells the story of a young, single mother from a small, southern town. She agrees to help unionize her textile mill despite the problems and dangers involved. Sally Fields wins her first of two best actress Academy Awards.

Erin Brockovich relates how an unemployed, single mother of three becomes a legal assistant and leads the case that brings down a California power company accused of polluting a city's water supply. Julia Roberts joined the "$20 million club" when she signed up for this role and earned an Oscar for her performance.

The modern culture of films reflects how women can lead society to a better life through activism. The Hollywood movie industry shows us that women's involvement in causes is rooted in their care for children's needs, family issues, and saving the environment. These movies illustrate activism's dangers, hard work, and lack of glamour. The battles of Norma and Erin were an organic outgrowth of their belief in a safer, more humane future.

CONNECTION: MENTORS

Nobody can be exactly like me. Even I have trouble doing it.
Tallulah Bankhead, Alabama-born actor

I've never been to New Zealand before. But one of my role models, Xena, the warrior princess, comes from there.
Madeleine Korbel Albright, first female Secretary of State

Connection is the elixir of cooperative leadership. A network of connections encourages collaborative efforts and lies at the heart of the leader/follower relationship. As leaders, we attend to detail and emotion and craft relationships where voices are heard and contributions valued. Women offer fresh perspectives on the role of cosmic connectedness in respectful, effective leadership.

Canadian writer Mavis Gallant captured one aspect of women dedicated to authentic leadership when she wrote, "She had the loaded handbag of someone who camps out and seldom goes home, or who imagines life must be full of emergencies." Women in leadership positions must step up to whatever comes and get the job done. Here is a story about a dynamic chief executive officer. Cynthia leads with an intuitive understanding of the power of connection and mentoring.

ᔆᕈ Challenging Message ᕈᔆ

An interview with a wild woman

Action oriented and strategic, Cynthia keeps her life vibrant by believing that we can find joy and happiness in relationships and hard work. Her message in a bottle to others: "Plan, do the work, and get it done," and "Believe in happy endings."

As president of a nonprofit organization dedicated to providing a program of physical, educational, and vocational guidance plus character-building activities for young children and adolescents, she rumbles with the thunder of frank, decisive leadership. Responsible for not one, but nine locations, she flashes with the lightening of clarity, confidence, and hard work. "I want to be a role model, trying to present the best I can be." Her mission: lead, develop others, and embrace diversity.

A postscript to the story: in one of my Creative Process classes at the University of Texas, I found someone whose life plans have been touched by Cynthia. The class assignment was to describe the dream job that would tap into their creative process. Carrie, one of my students, said she wanted to be an executive for a mental health agency. Her inspiration? Cynthia. My student had volunteered for Cynthia's organization and experienced first hand the dedication, intelligence, and caring Cynthia communicated to clients, staff, and volunteers. This twenty-something young woman aspired to a career that paralleled Cynthia's in leadership presence. Carrie said, "I want to be Cynthia when I grow up."

Productivity and morale become greater in atmospheres of trust-filled relational connection. Successful female leaders like Cynthia understand the importance of interpersonal connection. Cynthia lives as a prime example of how women can dispense support and respect and share success.

The affirming safe haven of effective woman-to-woman mentoring nurtures potential through interaction and encouragement. Mentoring, female style, offers meaningful, uplifting connections where strengths have the potential to be extended and liabilities can be defanged. The savvy navigational nudges of a mentor guide expanding talent, skill, and insight into confident harbors. Our fairy-goddess mentors listen respectfully and relate their own struggles. They communicate that others have dealt with the same issues and that success can be achieved in a number of ways. Preparing others for perhaps even greater performances, mentors get the added bonus of reviewing and refreshing their understanding of their work and accomplishments. By sharing knowledge and expertise, mentors gain new and broadened perspectives.

Our mentors travel with us for awhile and aid our journeys. Mentors lead with the gentle power of connection. Maeve Binchey, Irish novelist and journalist, communicated the essence of women's approach to mentoring. She wrote, "I don't have ugly ducklings turning into swans in my stories. I have ugly ducklings turning into confident ducks." Juliette Gordon Low understood confident ducks and role models. She was in her fifties when she discovered her life's passion and began her work on behalf of young girls. After meeting Sir Robert Baden-Powell, founder of the Boy Scouts and Girl Guides, Low translated these English scouting programs into an American version designed specifically for girls. Juliette Low wanted girls to have opportunities to learn about nature while developing readiness for traditional roles in addition to roles as professional women. Her goal for girls was to be prepared for active citizenship. In 1915, Girl Scouts of the USA was formally organized with Juliette Low as its founder and first president. The relational notions women bring to the world of leadership are personified in the very nature of mentoring. Low intuited the importance of nurturing young women and inspiring upcoming generations. She understood that mentoring is mutually motivating.

In the hands of women, mentoring can be more collaborative and cooperative than hierarchical. Mentoring fulfills its highest potential experienced as a relationship that both partners enjoy and learn from. The energy, resources, and strengths of both participants are engaged and energized. In mentoring partnerships women learn, develop, and derive satisfaction from working together. They support each other's development by providing outside perspectives. They share experiences, examples, information, and advice. They proffer the skills and model the proficiency that fortifies growth. Guided by the creative feminine, mentoring transforms emerging creativity and talent into productivity.

Let's travel to Hollywood again. The big screen visions of mentoring have been revealed in two more Academy Award-winning depictions of women in high-drama connection. Consider two stories about four women.

Chicago tells the story of Vaudeville star Velma Kelly and Vaudeville wannabee Roxie Hart. They meet in prison, where both are on death row for murder. In competition for best get-off-scot-free story, they do not hit it off. But, in best Hollywood tradition, they learn to share expertise. As the curtain goes up, the dancing duo brings the house down.

All About Eve spotlights Broadway legend Margo Channing and aspiring actor Eve Harrington as they meet in New York. Eve insinuates herself into Margo's life under the guise of a naïve, adoring fan and grateful student. As the story unfolds, we see Eve scheme to achieve success at Margo's expense. But in the best Hollywood tradition, retribution is close at hand. As the curtain comes down we see an ambitious ingénue humbly approaching Eve.

Hollywood portrayed capable and aspiring women as they shared potential for leading, learning, and succeeding. Two mentoring scenarios were depicted with very different outcomes. One concluded with a collaborative effort between equals, and the other depicted a flip-flop in success with comeuppance lurking in the wings. Women in mentoring relationships coach, care, share, and assist and at a deeper level explore their own determination and striving. Their wisdom, generosity, and support can be of mutual benefit and, as with life, sometimes full of unexpected results.

COURAGE: WARRIORS

I thought how unpleasant it is to be locked out; and I thought how it is worse, perhaps, to be locked in.
Virginia Stephen Woolf, British feminist, essayist, novelist

I am extraordinarily patient provided I get my own way in the end.
Margaret Thatcher, former UK prime minister, "The Iron Lady"

The word "courage" takes on a heightened meaning when applied to women. In general usage, "manly" is synonymous with courage, while "womanly" is synonymous with—you fill in the blank. Courageous women challenge the norm. There are many shibboleths attached to women and the ways that are open to them to demonstrate courage and leadership. The barometer hovers around nice, polite, and non-confrontational. Courage, power, and boldness play against stereotype and traditional contexts of hearth and home. Hermione Granger, a wand-toting, brio flashing wizard, exemplifies blasting courage simmering under a cloak of well-behaved and mannerly demeanor.

✑ Hermione Granger ✑

Never born, she will always live.

Hermione Granger is a fearless pursuer of knowledge. Best friend, Ron, says she is "brilliant, but scary." Her strong intellect makes mastering the art of wizardry seem easy. She has facts, answers, and solutions and is dauntless in her determination to share them. Hermione knows the rules and staunchly follows them precisely.

Hermione also is a daring wizard. She uses her brain to ingeniously bend the rules in support of friends. Need to gather secrets surreptitiously; Hermione can concoct a potion that transforms you into a confederate of the information holder. When the school bully starts needling Harry and Ron, it is Hermione who lands the punch that sends the bully on his way. Need someone to fight at your side and support you in life-threatening quests? With bravery beyond question and wand and fist at the ready, Granger's your go-to woman-at-arms.

—From the *Harry Potter* series created by J. K. Rowling, 1997

Hermione does not budge; she sticks with it no matter what. The women I admire most absolutely lead in the face of adversity; they stand up for family, country, and beliefs. My sort of uber-women use their courage to create, build, and defend. "If it's a good idea . . . go ahead and do it. It is much easier to apologize than it is to get permission," touted United States military leader and mathematician Grace Murray Hopper. Where my heroes see needs, they offer talent and leadership. Heroic women lead with courage in board rooms, executive suites, classrooms, hospitals, and battle fields. Women's courageous acts can and have made critical contributions to culture and civilization, successfully fighting injustice and the status quo.

Anita Hill, law professor, author, and public speaker, is best known for her resolute testimony in Clarence Thomas's Supreme Court Justice confirmation hearings. She articulated the essence of courageous action by saying, "I did what my conscience told me to do, and you can't fail if you do that." Courage supports female leaders as they reach beyond conventional, familiar, and comfortable responsibilities and roles. Great wit and frequent Algonquin visitor Dorothy Parker explained her courage to try the untried, "I don't know much about being a millionaire, but I bet I would be darling at it." You have got to love Dorothy, for surely she lived life on her own terms. The courage of such individuals pushes back on isolation, uncertainty, and complacency. The energy of powerful women generates determination in those who hear of their brave, trail-blazing exploits to make changes and take risks. Starchy backbones support passionate courage.

A fulfilled life requires daring to be true to ourselves. Gutsy women use courage to be clear about their identity and goals and their freedom to pursue their dreams. The tenacious leadership of the creative feminine taps, pushes, prods, and occasionally kicks us in the seat of the pants. Creativity and daring ideas tweak our courage and leadership prowess and encourage us to hack personal paths to the newest territories of goals and achievements.

Courage is not just for the big stuff. Women understand that courage pumps confidence, acknowledging and celebrating small successes. When a kindergarten teacher encourages a small child to take the risk of sounding out the letters, she knows that risk of failure is part of the hesitancy. But when C-A-T turns into "cat," courage transforms reserve into confidence and triumph. If C-A-T gets translated as "cut," courage urges another stab at those daunting three letters. Renowned primatologist Jane Goodall understood the desire that supports the courage to persist: "If you really want something, and really work hard, and take advantage of opportunities, and never give up, you will find a way." A dab of bravery allows us to regroup and try again.

Warrior-leaders are historically depicted as incredibly strong and occasionally scary. Looked at with fresh perspective, they model the feminine potential to transcend the present and create new and invigorated futures. Spitfire vitality and revved-up power symbolically illuminate our aspirations and inspire the courage to make them reality. Ferociously ingenious women wield steely courage, charisma, and wisdom.

In the 1950s, one courageous woman paved new ground for warrior women everywhere. Rosa Parks saw an opportunity to change things that were unjust and create better futures for others. On December 1, 1955, she refused to give up her bus seat to a white passenger. The bus driver had her arrested. Until that day, her statements against racism had been private. Rosa Parks had used the stairs rather than ride in a "blacks only" elevator and went thirsty rather than drink from a "colored only" water fountain.

Mrs. Parks waged a bold-spirited fight for civil rights, racial equality, and freedom. Her arrest and trial led to the 1956 Supreme Court ruling that segregation on public transportation is unconstitutional. Rosa Parks, warrior woman, increased life choices and inspired optimism. With great courage she defined her beliefs and backed them with action. In writing about Parks, civil rights activist, writer, history and law professor Mary Frances Berry explained, "If Rosa Parks had taken a poll before she sat down in the bus in Montgomery, she'd still be standing." Rosa brought a female-driven leadership perspective to world events. Radiant with ardor and command she let her vision-filled passion loose on the world. The impact of her courage enriched the abundance of future possibilities for humanity.

Courageous women exert the full power of leadership. Hermione Granger, Anita Hill, and Rosa Parks put on their mighty, creative energy shields and wielded their formidable creative strengths to change our world. They are touchstones in women's fight for educational, social, political, and economic equity. They show us a few of the paths women have traveled to improve lives and the quality of life.

COMMITMENT: ENVIRONMENTALISTS

When you realize the value of all life, you dwell less on what is past and concentrate more on the preservation of the future.

Dian Fossey, American zoologist

I've never quite believed that one chance is all I get.

Anne Tyler, Pulitzer Prize-winning author

As leaders, women are attuned to the need to arouse, build, and sustain commitment. We are aware that effective leaders inspire others and create enabling environments. Committed women encourage us to strive to attain something worthwhile and support our efforts. These remarkable role models remind us that we have a covenant with Mother Nature.

No matter the context, women can generate committed action for uplifting purpose and life affirming goals. Valorous women create environments that support passion, energy, and patience. Commitment inspired by the feminine creative highlights caring, safekeeping, and allegiance and places a deliberate emphasis on beneficial and practical priorities. Cherette exemplifies committed leadership when she acknowledges obligation and pledges to weather the storms of change with patients and students. She celebrates their willingness to risk and create successful change.

∽ **Keep Breathing** ∾

An interview with a wild woman

Cherette is deeply involved in a demanding, twofold work commitment. Being a family therapist and a yoga instructor taps the nurturing and caretaking she believes is the purpose of her work. The life of a family therapist specializing in domestic violence, her first chosen career, is exhilarating, exhausting, and full of creative possibilities. Her investment in these endeavors is rewarded when she sees the effects of her work on people's lives as they grow and change.

Cherette balances the mental concentration of therapy with her second chosen path, the physical discipline of yoga. Cherette tells both domestic violence survivors and yoga students to let go, trust their inner voices, invest in determination, and, most importantly, keep breathing. Out of the corner of her eye, she watches for the in-and-out of calm-restoring inhalation and exhalation.

Just as Cherette celebrates effort and healing for those she serves, women leaders assert the benefits of restoring and renewing our world. The world benefits from women's committed leadership styles. Women understand the spirit of commitment and its engaging, purposeful action. Anarchist Emma Goldman snapped out, "If I cannot dance, I want no part in your revolution." As leaders, women impel us to move forward and spur us on, urging us to be bold and colorful in our pursuits.

As the guardians of Mother Nature, environmentalists persuade us to attend to the air, water, and the very earth we depend upon. Wangari Maathai, Kenyan Nobel Peace Prize winner, knows that our planet is fragile and resources are limited. She shared this: "We need to promote development that does not destroy our environment." Environmentalists entreat us to observe, preserve, restore, and conserve natural resources. Take heed! Women serve as dynamic leaders in the world of ecology. They spearhead efforts to expose the environmental risks and hazards faced by planet Earth and all of her inhabitants. In preserving from extinction those who rely on a healthy, viable planet, women are torchbearers in the most crucial of human issues. Astute environmentalists create profound and ongoing change. Before we discerned the need for environmentalists, Harriet Beecher Stowe, American writer and abolitionist, wrote, "Women are the real architects of society." Women have observed the threats to our environment and have exposed and opposed poachers, despoilers, and all those who would drain Mother Nature of her resources and her ability to nurture.

Marjory Stoneman Douglas was called the Mother of the Everglades. Where others saw a worthless swamp, Marjory saw a magnificent river of grass and a unique resource that harbored a vital ecosystem. "It's women's business to be interested in the environment." Her passionate commitment to preserve and restore this ecological treasure stirred her to instigate the movement to declare the Everglades a national park. She would see the successful culmination of her efforts in 1947, when Harry Truman dedicated the Everglades National Park. In 1993, Stoneman was awarded the Presidential Medal of Freedom—the highest honor awarded a civilian. She died in 1998 at 108.

Women who devote their lives to understanding humanity's connections to nature are zealous guardians of our environment. Count on these powerhouses to actively strive for changes to ensure a healthier planet. Women environmentalists prompt us to use Earth's abundant riches wisely and alert us to threats that imperil the climate, oceans, forests, and animals. As effective leaders they work to slow the destruction of the environment by assessing and using their expertise to press for informed action and constructive change.

In 1997, Julia Butterfly Hill climbed into a 180-foot California Redwood to save it from destruction by loggers. She sat in the tree, known as Luna, for 738 days to protect it and the surrounding 1,000-year-old forest. Julia Butterfly Hill went out on a limb to promote the sustainability, restoration, and preservation of life. Meaning only to sit for one night, her two-year vigil demonstrated her belief in the interconnectedness of all living things. She says, "After I came down from living in that tree, I realized how literally every moment we make choices and every single choice changes the world—every single one of them." Julia is the youngest person to be inducted into the Ecology Hall of Fame.

Women, like Julia, are attuned to the care and study of humankind and our habitat. Their environmental contributions work toward saving nature and making the planet safe for its inhabitants. As committed leaders passionate about our planet, women have exposed health and environmental risks and identified endangered species and threats to our ecological system.

As creative spirits, each of us can commit energy, effort, and expertise to support the survival of Great Lady Nature. Dedicated to saving our planet for all living things, fierce guardians have offered altruistic and thoughtful leadership. Environmentalists study and work on behalf of planet earth and all of her inhabitants.

From the voices of the more than forty women included in this chapter, a few common themes emerge. These women who made a difference know their own minds, are delighted to share their thoughts and beliefs, and have a way with words and a penchant for taking purposeful action. These creative dynamos epitomize the power of vision, connection, courage, and commitment and display the full power of their feminine creative. As a group, these diverse leaders are, or were, willing to put themselves on the line to pave the way for a better future. As far as I know, only one carried a magic wand.

Chapter Eight

Women Preside

You only live once, but if you do it right, once is enough.

— Mae West, irreverent and whimsical bombshell

Life should be lived so lively and so intensely that thoughts of another life, or of a longer life, are not necessary.

—Majory Stoneman Douglas, journalist, environmentalist

*H*ow do we nurture our creative spirits? How do we become goddesses, guardians, innovators, inspirers, leaders, trailblazers, instigators, and beguilers? Read on.

Here is the best news ever: Creativity comes more easily than most other human traits. Remember, it is enhanced through awareness and use. There are lots of other good human qualities, but they often need practice. You know the old, use-or-lose-it adage? Not so, with creativity. Just like the blinking cursor on the screen of life, creativity waits to have you click in and whiz along. Pay a little attention to creativity, and it responds. Indulge your creative appetite; feed it gummy bears, Tootsie Rolls, and potato chips. Say yes, yes, yes, and, and, and, and. You will find this approach is easier, and more fun, than no and not. So, what am I suggesting? Entertain your creative feminine, and spoil her rotten. When in doubt add something to your life rather than take something away.

I love my creativity, and I like to keep her fat, happy, and sassy. I love to say yes. I have always loved adding and never cared much for taking away. I remember learning addition as a first grader, counting up the columns of numbers and getting a bigger number. When you subtracted, the answer got smaller. Boo, hiss. When big time addition and subtraction came along, we got to carry in addition and borrow in subtraction. Borrowing and take away still seem narrow and mingy to me. Carrying reminds me of bringing home something wonderful in a shopping bag.

We are creative by nature, so we live creatively. Our creativity brings whimsy that is expressed in our unique style according to our own brew of nature and nurture. We fall in love and make friends. We learn, achieve, and lead in our own special way. How great is that? Here is more good news. Creativity is a great habit to cultivate. The more we use it, the more ingrained it becomes in our brain and way of life. One more blissful thought: creativity is highly contagious. So make it a habit to hang out with folks who say things like, "of course we can," "I wonder if," "let's flip it around and try it this way," or "I have a great idea." Don't hesitate to share your creativity with others. Get out there and spread it around.

SO WHAT AND HOW SO?

Life is what we make it, always has been, always will.
Anna Mary Robertson Moses, a.k.a. Grandma Moses,
American folk artist

Lead me not into temptation, I can find the way myself.
Rita Mae Brown, American author, playwright

Creativity is not limited to the privileged or artistically gifted. We all have it.

So what? Creativity improves the quality of life, relationships, work, play, and the world. Creativity engenders new ways of looking, seeing, and understanding, as well as diverse ways of making what we want real. It layers our own weird, wonderful, wacky, oddball, and rare emphasis onto everything we do, learn, and achieve. We cannot do it like anybody else, even if we try. Have you ever gotten a recipe from a friend? Does it ever come out exactly the same? No, and that's true even if your friend is Rachael Ray. My brother John, my sister Gina, and I, all make Mom's gumbo, but let me tell you, we create three very different bowls of New Orleans' finest.

How so? Creativity is uniquely and peculiarly human. Each of us possesses our personal stash. What stimulates and excites this wonderful gift, and how we express it, is singularly our own. Talents, experiences, challenges, families, chromosomes, and hormones nudge us. We all live, connect, learn, achieve, and lead in diverse styles that take us in distinctive directions.

Connect

If we fail to nourish our souls, they wither, and without soul, life ceases to have meaning. The creative process shrivels in the absence of continual dialogue with the soul. And creativity is what makes life worth living.
Marion Woodman, Jungian analyst, author

What the world really needs is more love and less paperwork.
Pearl Bailey, composer, singer

Lovers of life and creativity extend all-important human connections. They instigate parties, family reunions, and get-togethers. We want warmth, and a dollop of intimacy never hurt anybody. We can be scholars, achievers, and leaders and still be wives, partners, mothers, and providers of emotional support. Remember, I like the word "and!" Women bring their relational talents to life with their creativity. I passionately believe that deeply creative women shape lifestyles that encourage connections with people and maintain authentic relationships. I am convinced creative women invent as many methods of mothering as they have angles on marriage and mating. As far as I can tell, there is no singularly transcendent or remarkably uncomplicated approach. We live life our way.

Isadora Duncan had a deep appreciation for the feminine nature of the universe. She intuited that creativity was a part of something larger than herself and that the fruits of creativity conjured beauty and emotional aliveness. Fashion iconoclast Sarah Jessica Parker might have been channeling a dash of Isadora when she shared her own brand of free spirit. "I don't judge others. I say if you feel good with what you're doing, let your freak flag fly." Isadora lived and danced her whole life in cahoots with unorthodox non-conformity. She was always an adventurer and forever a nurturer of the poetic spirit and the creative ethos.

Isadora's personal life was flamboyantly individualistic and progressive. She flouted traditional mores and defied social taboos. She believed in free love and lived life accordingly. She was married and divorced, had two children with two specifically chosen men, and had numerous lovers. Duncan applied this same avant-garde approach to her union with movement and music that was to give birth to modern dance.

As the mother of modern dance, Isadora moved from conservative classical conventions into modern expressive interpretations. As an innovator, she rejected traditional dance structures. Instead, she stressed improvisation, emotion, and the human body. She was the fountainhead of an original and singular form of dance. She traced dance's roots back to classical Greece and then incorporated the panache of American athleticism including walking, skipping, running, and jumping.

Duncan had little formal training and did not need any. Isadora relied on her graceful style and flowing energy. Isadora repudiated artificial restrictions and drew from natural body movement. "If I could tell you what it meant, there would be no point in dancing it," related Isadora about the meaning of her unrestrained dance. She danced with vitality, insight, and talent. For Isadora, passionate dance was a personification of poetry and music and an emotional response to life.

Her unfettered and easy animation embodied the essence of her dance and choreography. Free-flowing costumes, bare feet, and loose hair were essential elements. Isadora's dancing was a celebration of simplicity, daring, and resourcefulness. As a choreographic innovator with an intuitive sense of the dynamics of mobility, she could add the right touch with nuances and subtleties of gesture. Duncan believed, "To dance is to live."

Learn

Don't let anyone rob you of your imagination, your creativity, or your curiosity. It's your place in the world; it's your life. Go on and do all you can with it, and make it the life you want to live.
Mae Jemison, M.D., astronaut, professor

Look at everything as though you were seeing it either for the first or last time. Then your time on earth will be filled with glory.
Betty Smith, author

Women have opened the doors of education for women, and those with a hunger for information are showing up for school like it's a 90-percent-off sale at the shopping mall. Education gives creativity a big fat boost, so keep on learning. Lifelong learners are those ever-curious seekers who love to wrestle with new ideas. You can spot them in classrooms, seminars, bookstores, and libraries as they search for enlightenment. Online they research, surf, and blog. For these techno-learners, the scoop, the low down, and the latest are only a few clicks away.

Like many a confirmed and abiding learner, Edith Head never let an opportunity to innovate or acquire new skills pass her by. Edith's formal education and career experience were impressive. She had a master's degree from Stanford University and taught French and art at an exclusive high school. Now here is where the additive value of creativity paid off. Edith wanted higher pay and something a little more exciting. Did she try to get a better paying job in education? No way! With no expertise or experience in costume design, she applied for a job in the costume department at Paramount Studio. She brought a very sketchy portfolio of her work, and, lo and behold, she got the job. Edith learned her new job on the job. She grasped the magic it took to cut and drape fabric in a way that transformed sagging breasts, big bottoms, thick waists, scrawny necks, and skinny arms. Bette Davis, Audrey Hepburn, Dorothy Lamour, Elizabeth Taylor, Grace Kelly. Can you connect the body part with the name? I'm not telling.

"A designer is only as good as the star who wears her clothes," Edith declared. During her long career, she created fashion images for famous actresses and actors that would be seen and emulated by millions. Head defined glamour in the glamour capitol of the world. For six decades she reigned supreme in Hollywood, was nominated for thirty-six Oscars, and won eight, more than any other woman has received.

Fearless learners trek uncharted territory. Seasoned seekers of knowledge weather the unknown and sample whatever comes along. Intrepid in their search, they incorporate new experiences and use them to strengthen thinking and nurture creativity.

Achieve

My eyes are an ocean in which my dreams are reflected.
Anna M. Uhlich, author

I promoted my self. I had to make my own opportunity! But I made it! Don't sit down and wait for opportunities to come.
Sarah Breedlove Walker, American millionaire, inventor

Lee Krasner was a smart woman in an era that denied women's choices, talents, and independence. Her dream was to be a full-time professional artist. She was a serious student and an ambitious painter. Lee worked at her art and was never afraid to reinvent and recreate.

As an ever-evolving abstract expressionist, she was headstrong, independent, and rigorously self-critical. Lee's discerning eye and keen judgment inspired her to periodically revise earlier efforts and occasionally destroy whole bodies of work. Krasner would cut out sections of her earlier works to create collages. She found freedom from constraint and was able to reinvent her own art.

Lee's drive to improve, nurture, enrich, and extend her creative ability is palpable in her vibrant and life-affirming work. Just like her, other achievers and hard workers dig in. They love getting the tough jobs done and cannot wait for the next challenge. Women work because we want to and because economically we need to. The possibility of financial independence is a modern reality in most of the Western world. Just like a former generation's conviction that father knows best, and wait until your father gets home, and man as the sole financial supporter of a family were reality, accepted truths can fade away like an old Polaroid snapshot.

This generation's single women, single mothers, and women with husbands and families step in, step up, bring home the bacon, and fry it up for breakfast. Today's force of women have opened up careers and realized more options and better pay. Just dipping our toes into the world of work does not work much anymore and is a rare occurrence these days. Ever-creative women are driven by a need to work, and a strong work ethic has led to more women becoming financially able to buy homes and own businesses. Hard-working Martha Stewart says, "That's a good thing." And as Bella Abzug, feminist pacifist, asserted, "The test for whether or not you can hold a job should not be the arrangement of your chromosomes." I like the picture of Martha and Bella gabbing together about women. How 'bout you?

Women recognize that our life's work, just like life itself, is a personal, handcrafted endeavor. Our creative feminine cheers us on as we move away from rigid alternatives and create personal combinations. Why settle for a taco when we can have the whole enchilada of work, career, relationship, education, and life? Yes we can, and yes we do. Who is to say if it's a soup, a stew, or mishmash? We create with the power of seat-of-the-pants innovation and thoughtfully informed strategy. With the artful grace of a poet, psychoanalyst Clarissa Pinkola Estés wrote, "I hope you will go out and let stories happen to you, and that you will work them, water them with your blood and tears and laughter till they bloom, till you yourself burst into bloom."

Lead

*It is good to have an end to journey toward, but it is the journey
that matters in the end.*
Ursula K. Le Guin, science fiction author

*Leadership should be born out of the understanding of the needs
of those who would be affected by it.*
Marian Anderson, opera star, United Nations ambassador

We must have leaders, crusaders, and fighters who feel the drive
to challenge the status quo, fight the norm, expose bias and inequity,
and improve worlds. I am not a fearless crusader, but I am thankful
for women who are. They keep doors that have been opened open,
and then they open some more. These women are demanding. They
have asked for, and earned, a growing equality in wages and opportunities. They bring the female voice into government. They fight
for freedom of artistic expression. They ask for what they want and,
if they do not get it, they follow up with action.

Women, the lodestars of opportunity and choice, touch life's
endeavors with the mega-watt voltage of "yes" plus "and." Yoko Ono
leads a life of "affirmatives" and "definitelys" with many an "also" and
"furthermore" thrown in. Ono is a world class fighter and world
famous lover. She faces controversy, opposition, and censorship by
digging deeply into her creative feminine to find strength and new
inspirations. As an artistic visionary, she infuses her films, concerts,
and albums with uncompromising and uncommon perspectives.

Rock music icon, performance artist, and avant-garde musician only begin to capture Yoko's range of creative expression. Ono channels her creative spirit with unflinching conviction. "I deal with the music of the mind," she says. In her eighth decade, she remains an influential force in the world of creativity and still courts her bounteous, diverse, and offbeat creative feminine. In her latest venture, Yoko released *Yes, I'm A Witch*, a remix album. The artists invited to contribute were allowed to select any song from Ono's back catalog and were given complete freedom to reinterpret and remix. The artists keep Yoko's vocals and create new backing tracks. Her vocal style and lyrical compositions were synced up with modern pop musicians. Yoko Ono, ocean child, continues to seek a unique angle and sound a resonant chord.

WOMEN PRESIDE!

Cherish forever what makes you unique, 'cuz you're really a yawn if it goes.
Bette Midler, The Divine Miss M

To love what you do and feel that it matters—how can anything be more fun?
Katharine Graham, American publisher

Women preside! Have fun, celebrate your life, and fall in love with your creative feminine. Let your enthusiasm loose on the world. Passionately embrace the cosmos; scrupulously attend to the world. Different seasons of life and beckoning divergent paths influence choices. Stay open to the myriad passages that life presents. Always be ready to enrich life. Remain on the lookout for the beautiful, elegant, expedient, and versatile.

My parting advice to all you wild women out there: occupy a place of authority, a place where your creative feminine is allowed to rule and run free. My favorite seat of authority is a green beach chair settled on a specific happy stretch of white sand. There, my wild woman revels in the freedom of timeless and unfettered creative space. The clear, blue water ripples in and out, forever clearing away footprints and renewing inspiration. The ever-balanced horizon calms my soul and stirs my brain. While I write these words, I must call my fingers, heart, and soul back to the keyboard. In all but this empty shell of a body, I am already on the beach.

References

Aboriginal Peoples Family Accord. "Grandmothers."
http://www.apfabc.org/grandmothers.htm. (accessed 9 July 2004).

Ackerman, Diane. *An Alchemy of Mind: The Marvel and Mystery of the Brain*. New York: Scribner, 2004.

"A Definition of Community."
http://muextension.missouri.edu/xplor/miscpubs/mp0568.htm.
(accessed 6 July 2004).

"Advice on Divorce Rates – What You Should Know."
http://www.marriage-relationships.com/divorce_rates.html.
(accessed 6 July 2004).

"Aesthetic." http://www.ananyadancetheatre.org/aesthetic.htm. (accessed 28 June 2007).

"Alice B. Toklas." http://en.wikipedia.org/wiki/Alice_B._Toklas.
(accessed 9 February 2007).

"Amazons." http://www.geocite.com/Wellesley/1582/amazons.html. (accessed 11 September 2004).

"Ani DiFranco." http://www.music.msn.com/artist/?=16100363&contenttype=bio. (accessed 26 January 2007).

Baber, Kristine and Katherine Allen. *Women and Families: Feminist Reconstructions.* New York: Guilford Press, 1992.

Baumgardner, Jennifer and Amy Richards. "What is Feminism?" 2000, http://www. feminist.com/resources/artspeech/genwom/whatisfem.htm. (accessed 21 April 2004).

Bedi, J. E. "Exploring the History of Women Inventors." http://invention.smithsonian.org/centerpieces/ilives/womeninventors.html. (accessed 17 January 2007).

Belilove, Lori. "About Isadora Duncan." http://www.isadoraduncan.org/about_isadora.html. (accessed 23 March 2007).

Bird, Patrick. "Keeping Fit" 1991, http://www.hhp.ufl.edu/keepingfit/ARTICLE/life.htm. (accessed 3 March 2004).

Block, Lory. "Finding Significance in Your Work." http://www.womentodaymagazine.com/career/sigwork.html. (accessed 10 September 2004).

Block, Naomi. "The Empowerment of Women." http://www.elderhostel.org/Ein/empowerment.asp. (accessed 10 September 2004).

"Bonnie Parker: a Gangster in Love." http://www.suite101.com/article.cfm/historys_wild_women/85305. (accessed 20 February 2007).

Brizendine, Louann. *The Female Brain.* New York: Random House, Inc. 2006.

Brunner, Borgina. "The History of Women's History." http://www.infoplease.com/spot/womensintro1.html. (accessed 17 June 2003).

References

Bruccoli, M. J., Smith, Scottie Fitzgerald, and Kerr, Joan P., eds. 1975. The Romantic Egoists: *A Pictorial Autobiography from the Scrapbooks and Albums of Scott and Zelda Fitzgerald*. New York: Charles Scribner's Sons.

"Brown Foundation." http://brownvboard.org/foundation/. (accessed 15 February 2007).

"Calamity Jane." http://www.infoplease.com/ce6/people/A0809840.html. (accessed 23 January 2007).

Cardillo, Maren. "Intimate Relationships: Personality Development Through Interaction During Early Life." http://www.personalityresearch.org/papers/cardillo.html. (accessed 7 June 2004).

"Career Stages." http://www.bc.edu_org/avp/wfnetwork/rft/wfpedia/efpCSent.html. (accessed 29 May 2004).

"Career Volunteering." http://playlab.uconn.edu/stebbins2.htm. (accessed 20 September 2004).

Casto, Michelle. "The Characteristics of Highly Creative People. " http://enchanted spirit.org/Potpourri/191.php. (accessed 12 September 2003).

CeMCOR: the Centre for Menstrual Cycle and Ovulation Research. "Women's Life Stages – Adolescence – What's Normal? What Can Go Wrong?" 2003. http://www.cemcor.ubc.ca/lifestages/adolescence/normal.shtml. (accessed 26 February 2004).

Chipman, Dawn. *Cool Women: The Thinking Girl's guide to the Hippest Women in History*. Chicago: Girl Press. 2001.

Christie, Agatha. *The Murder at the Vicarage*. New York: Dodd, Mead & Company. 1930.

"Creative Play". http://www.pbs.org/wholechild/providers/play.htm. (accessed 4 October 2004).

"Depression-Era Duet." http://www.crimelibrary.com/americana/bonnie/main.htm. (accessed 10 February 2007).

Duncan, Isadora." http://search.eb.com/women/article-9031459. (accessed 23 March 2007).

Dye, David. "Yoko Ono: More Than a Beatle's Widow." http://www.npr.org/templates/story/story.php?storyId=7453636. (accessed 19 March 2007).

"Ecology Hall of Fame: Julia Butterfly Hill." http://www.ecotopia.org/ehof/hill/index.html. (accessed 10 March 2007).

"Edith Head." http://en.wikipedia.org/wiki/Edith_Head. (accessed 14 March 2007).

"Edith Head." http://www.otis.edu/alumni/da/ehead.htm. (accessed 14 March 2007).

Eisenberg, Bonnie and Mary Ruthsdotter. "Living the Legacy: The Women's Rights Movement 1848 – 1998." http://www.legacy98.org/move-hist.html. (accessed 22 October 2003).

"Elizabeth Cady Stanton." http://en.wikipedia.org/wiki/Elizabeth_Cady_Stanton. (accessed 18 January 2007).

Entenmann, Dalene. "The Creativity of Our Being." http://www.hopeandhealing.com/creativity-of-being.htm. (accessed 8 September 2003).

"Female Inventors." http://www.inventions.org/culture/female/jacob.html. (accessed 17 January 2007).

"Friendships Between Women." http://www.boadachia.com/new_age/friendships_women.htm. (accessed 5 July 2004).

"Gertrude and Alice." http://www.salon.com/mwt/feature/1999/11/18/alice/index.html. (accessed 9 February 2007).

"Goddesses." http://www.geocite.com/Wellesley/1582/goddesses.html. (accessed 11 September 2004).

Gordon, Linda. "The "New" U.S. Women's History (1)." http://www.womenof.com?Articles/p032299.asp. (accessed 6 July 2004).

Hewlett, Sylvia Ann. "Executive Women and the Myth of Having It All." 2002. Harvard Business Review, April 2002.

References

"History of Marriage: An Interview with Stephanie Coontz." Family Therapy Magazine. Jan-Feb 2004. pp 19-25.

"Human Relationships." http://academic.cuesta.edu/sguglielmo/Relationships.htm. (accessed 5 July 2004).

Illinois Department of Aging. "Life Expectancy for Women." Slide 103, June 30, 2000, http://www.uic.edu/orgs/rin/2000rpt/ch8/sld103.htm. (accessed 3 March 2004).

"Isadora Duncan." http://en.wikipedia.org/wiki/Isadora_Duncan. (accessed 23 March 2007).

Jackson, Denny. "Biography for Mary Pickford." http://imdb.com/name/nm0681933/bio. (accesssed 22 March 2007).

James, Louise Boyd. "From Coast to Coast." http://accelerateu.org/assessments/Ela8/FromCoasttoCoast,htm. (accessed 1 July 2007).

"Jeanne Calment." http://en.wikipedia.org/wiki/Jeanne_Calment. (accessed 28 March 2007).

"Julia Butterfly Hill." http://www.lupec.org/events/2004/nvironmentalists/index.html. (accessed 3 March 2007).

"Juliette Gordon Low." http://www.georgiaencyclopedia.org/nge/Article.jsp?id=h-2893. (accessed 2 March 2007).

"Knowing Nancy Drew." http://nancy-drew.mysterynet.com/nancydrew/grownups/nancy/evolution.shtml. (accessed 4 August 2005).

Larson, Ruth, "Gender Gap Dooms Men to Shorter Life Spans." Insight on the News, June 7, 1999. http://www.findarticles.com/cf_dls1571/21_15/54852031/p1/article.jhtml. (accessed 9 March 2004).

"Leadership." http://www.jefallbright.net/leadership. (accessed 3 March 2004).

"Lee Krasner." http://en.wikipedia.org/wiki/Lee_Krasner. (accessed 15 March 2007).

"Lee Krasner." http://naples.cc.sunysb.edu/CAS/pkhouse.nsf/pages/krasner. (accessed 15 March 2007).

Le Van, Alicia. "The Gorgon Medusa."
http://www.persues.tufts.edu/classes/finALp.html. (accessed 23 September 2004).

"Linda Brown Thompson."
http://www.pbs.org/kcet/publicschool/innovators/brown.html. (accessed 15 February 2007).

"Liquid Paper – Bette Nesmith Graham (1922-1980)."
http://inventors.about.cpm/od/lstartinventions/a/liquid_pper.htm. (accessed 27 January 2007).

"Louise Berliawsky Nevelson"
http://en.wikipedia.org/wiki/Louise_Nevelson. (accessed 22 March 2007).

"Mae Jemison."
http://school.discovery.com/schooladventures/womenofthecentury/phenomenalwomen/spaceandscience.htm. (accessed 14 March 2007).

"Maggie Kuhn." http://en.wikipedia.org/wiki/Maggie_Kuhn. (accessed 13 February 2007).

"Make New Friends But Keep The Old."
http://ww.urbanext.uiuc.edu/mclean/family/newfriends.html. (accessed 6 July 2004).

"Maria Mitchell: Historical Eclipse Chaser."
http://physicsandastronomy.vasser.edu/mariamitchell/. (accessed 13 February 2007).

"Marjory Stoneman Douglas."
http://www.pajaritoee.org/3a_nature_guide/ecologist_ng.htm. (accessed 8 March 2007).

"Marjory Stoneman Douglas."
http://www.wellesley.edu?Anniversary/douglas.html. (accessed 8 March 2007).

"Mary Anderson."
http://inventors.about.com/library/inventors/blanderson.htm. (accessed 27 January 2007).

"Mary Harris (Mother) Jones: c. 1837-1930."
http://digital.library.upenn.edu/women/jones/MotherJones.html. (accessed 3 March 2007).

Miller, Jean Baker. Toward a New Psychology of Women. 2nd ed. Boston: Beacon Press. 1986.

References

Miller, Laura. "Ain"t I a Woman?"
http://dir.salon.com/story/opinion/freedom/2003/07/29/sojourner_truth/index.
html. (accessed 24 January 2007).

"Mission." http://www.ananyadancetheatre.org/Mission.htm. (accessed 28 June 2007).

Mitchell, Margaret. Gone With the Wind. New York: The MacMillan Company. 1936.

"Molly Ivins." http://www.freepress.org/columns/display/1. (accessed 22 March 2007).

"Nancy Brinker." http://en.wikipedia.org/wiki/Nancy_Brinker. (accessed 7 February 2007).

Naranjo-Huebl, Linda. "From Peek-a-boo to Sarcasm: Women's Humor as a Means
of Both Connection and Resistance."
http://www.fnsa.org/v1n4/huebl1.html. (accessed 18 September 2003).

"Older Women: Key Intergenerational Figures."
http://www.penpages.psu.edu/penpages_reference/21600/21600477.HTML.
(accessed 5 July 2004).

"Passion: What You Want from Life."
hhtp://www.soulmaking.com/careerinward.htm. (accessed 30 September 2004).

Pernoud, Régine. "Eleanor of Aquitaine."
http://search.eb.com/women/print?articleId=32256&fullArticle+true&tocI
d+9032256. (accessed 23 March 2007).

Quindlin, Anna. 1997. "Life in the 30s." Keynote address presented at the annual
conference for the National Association of Independent Schools, February 26 –
March 1 in San Francisco, California.

Robinson, Dawn and Smith-Lovin, Lynn. "Getting a Laugh: Gender, Status, and
Humor in Task Discussion." Social Forces. Vol. 80.No. 1. Pp123-158.

Rochlin, Margy. "Diane Keaton's Slant on Life." More. February 2007. Pp92-96 and p188.

Rodriguez, Alicia. "Women's Style of Leadership Gets Noticed."
http://www.sclmcoach.com/leadership.html. (accessed 6 July 2004).

"Rosa Parks." http://www.achievement.org/autodoc/page/par0bio-1 (accessed 4 March 2007).

Women Create!

"Rosa Parks, Mother of the Civil Rights Movement."
http://www.girlpower.gov/girlarea/gpguests/RosaParks.htm. (accessed 24 March).

"Rose Fitzgerald Kennedy." http://www.wic.org/rkennedy.htm (accessed 1 March 2007).

Rosenberg, Matt, "Life Expectancy," About Geography, 2004,
http://geography.about.com/library/weekly/aa042000a.htm. (accessed 3
March 2004).

Russo, Jennifer, "A Woman's Response to Stress." iVillage, June 6, 2000.
http://www.ivillagehealth.com/interests/women/articles/0,,416898_249533,00.htm.
(accessed 10 March 2004).

"Sandra Day O'Connor."
http://www.gale.com/free_resources/whm/bio/oconnor_s.htm. (accessed 21
February 2007).

Schulman, Lisa. "Nancy Drew, Beloved Heroine" from "Knowing Nancy Drew,"
Newfront Productions, 1998.
http://nancydrew.mysterynet.com/nancydrew/grownups/nancy/owe.shtml.
(accessed 4 August 2005).

"Science & Puberty."
http://www.exmuslim.com/com/science_&_puberty.htm. (accessed 20 April 2004).

Sheehy, Gail. New Passages. New York: Random House, 1995.

Shlain, Leonard. *Sex, Time and Power: How Women's Sexuality Shaped Human Evolution*.
New York: Viking, 2003.

Schlegel, Margaret. "Women Mentoring Women."
http://www.apa.org/monitor/nov00/mentoring.html. (accessed 5 July 2004).

Shiffman, Ron and Shiffman, Yvette. "Creativity Collage."
http://www.picced.org/resources/sc983.htm. (accessed 20 August 2003).

"Skateboarding." http://en.wikipedia.org/wiki/Skateboarding. (accessed 2
February 2007).

Steinem, Gloria. *Outrageous Acts and Everyday Rebellions*. New York: Holt, Rinehart
and Winston. 1983.

References

Taylor, S.E., Klien, L.C., Lewis, B.P., Gruenewald, T.L., Garung, R.A.R., and Updegraff, J.A. "Women & Friendship" http://studenthealth.oregonstate.edu/Health_News_Events/Women&Friendship. htm. (accessed 9 April 2004).

"The Feminine Touch." http://www.ingenuitynews.co.za/bookmark.htm. (accessed 17 January 2007).

"The Founder of Mothers Day." http://www.rootsweb.com/~wvtaylor/founder.htm. (accessed 8 February 2007).

TheFreeDictionary.com. "Feminism." http://encyclopedia.thefreedictionary.com/feminism. (accessed 20 April 2004).

The Importance of Play." http://www.instituteforplay.com/5importance_of-play.htm. (accessed 20 September 2004).

"The Kennedys." http://www.pbs.org/wgbh/amex/kennedys/peopleevents/p_rose.html (accessed 1 March 2007).

"Theodora (6th century)." http://en.wikipedia.org/wiki/Theodora_(6th_century. (accessed 21 June 2007).

"The Promise of Play." http://www.instituteforplay.com/2promise_of_play.htm. (accessed 20 September 2004).

Thomas, Pauline Weston. "Bras and Girdles Before 1950." http://www.fashion-era.com/bras_and_girdles.htm. (accessed 9 June 2004).

Thomas, Pauline Weston. "Theories of Fashion: Costume and Fashion History." http://www.fashion-era.com/sociology_semiotics.htm. (accessed 9 June 2004).

University of California Los Angeles, College of Letters & Science. "UCLA Researchers Identify Key Biobehavioral Pattern Used by Women to Manage Stress." http://www.college.ucla.edu/stress.htm. (accessed 10 March 2004).

University of Dayton Women's Center. http://womenscenter.udayton.edu/programs/. (accessed 14 September 2004).

Vaillant, George E., M.D. Aging Well. Boston: Little, Brown and Company. 2002.

"Volunteerism." http://iml.umkc.edu/casww/sa/Volunteerrism.htm. (accessed 10 September 2004).

"Wallenda, Helen Kries." http://www.findagrave.com/cgi-bin/fg.cgi?page=gr&GRid=13209917. (accessed 24 February 2007).

Wallenda, Tino. "The Flying Wallendas." http://www.wallenda.com/history.html. (accessed 24 February 2007).

"What is Fashion?" http://www.fashion-era.com/sociology_semiotics.htm. (accessed 9 June 2004).

White, Martha. "Creativity and the Learning Culture." The Learning Organization, September 1994, http://www.ibsail.com/creativi.htm. (accessed 13 February 2004).

"Women in Minoan Culture." http://www.wsu.edu/~dee/MONOA/WOMEN.HTM. (accessed 19 February 2007).

"Women Inventors." http://www.enchantedlearning.com/inventors/women.shtml. (accessed 17 January 2007.

"Women's Career Development." http://www.penpages.psu.edu/penpages_references/28507/285072923.HTML. (accessed 29 May 2004).

"Women of the Hall." http://www.greatwomen.org/women.php?action=viewone&id=62. (accessed 25 January 2007).

"Women of the Hall." http://www.greatwomen.org/women.php?action=viewone&id=89. (accessed 3 March 2007).

"Women Working in the Media." http://www.media-awareness.ca/english/issues/stereotyping/women_and_girls/women. (accessed 24 June 2007).

References

Wonder Woman."
http://ww.bbc.co.uk/science/hottopics/superheroes/wonderwoman.shtml.
(accessed 7 April 2004).

World Health Organization. "Women, Ageing and Health." Fact sheet Number 252,
June 2000. http://www.who.int/mediacentre/factsheets/fs252/en/print.html.
(accessed 3 March 2004).

"Yoko Ono." http://www.nndb.com/people/087/000023018. (accessed 19 March 2007).